There Is No Rose

There Is No Rose

The Mariology of the Catholic Church

Aidan Nichols, OP

Fortress Press
Minneapolis

THERE IS NO ROSE
The Mariology of the Catholic Church

The author and publisher are grateful to the Eparchy of Saskatoon and the Liturgical Commission of the Synod of the Hierarchy of the Ukrainian Catholic Church for permission to cite from their approved translations of respectively, 'Acathistos in honor of Christ the Lover of Mankind and Blessed Virgin Mary' (Saskatoon, 1981)and 'The Sacred and Divine Liturgy of our Holy Father John Chrsyostom (Philadelphia, 1987)

Cover image: Our Lady of Korsum by Russian icon/17th century/Super Stock
Cover design: Laurie Ingram

Library of Congress Cataloging-in-Publication Data
Print ISBN: 978-1-4514-8446-5
eBook ISBN: 978-1-4514-9416-7

The paper used in this publication meets the minimum requirements of American National Standard for Information Sciences — Permanence of Paper for Printed Library Materials, ANSI Z329.48-1984.

Manufactured in the U.S.A.

This book was produced using PressBooks.com, and PDF rendering was done by PrinceXML.

There is no rose of such virtue

As is the Rose that bare Jesu

—Medieval English carol

Contents

Preface

In the course of the last century, the ideas of Catholic theologians about Mary shifted startlingly. Neo-Scholastic Mariology, with its robust metaphysics, sought chiefly to describe the unique status of the woman who was the Mother of the Word of God incarnate, equipped for her role, and her wider destiny, by special supernatural "privileges." The biblically oriented Mariological writing which prepared the way for, and followed on, the Second Vatican Council (1962–1965) was more concerned with Mary's exemplary status as a woman of faith. This approach, in itself perfectly legitimate (not least, it was a common theme of the ancient Fathers of the church), could morph into something rather more ideological at the hands of some writers for whom the claims for the Mother of God typical of classical Catholic doctrine and traditional devotion were thrown into the shade—to put it kindly. Somewhere between these two sharply contrasted approaches (and midway between them in time) lay the path of a *ressourcement* theology which, in "returning to sources" not only scriptural but also liturgical and patristic, sought to enrich the inheritance of Latin theology by adding an emphasis that was more *cordial*—addressing the "existential" dimension proper to persons and prosecuting its task not only in the categories of ontology but in the language of the heart.

The present study aims to contribute to the revival of a more full-blooded body of Marian teaching, taking its cue from, especially, the major encyclical letter of John Paul II, *Redemptoris mater*, issued in 1987. In the way proper to a Catholic theologian (of any period) I seek here to synthesize biblical data with resources from the subsequent tradition. And in the spirit of a pope who was both poet and philosopher, I exclude neither the materials of tradition in its imagistic mode, as with much of the celebration of Mary's role found in the Fathers and the liturgies, nor the deliverances of tradition in its more conceptual manner, as in the great assertions of the councils and the magisterium of the popes, commented and explained as these are by the church's divines, not least via the argumentative strategies of the Scholastics, notably St Thomas and the members of his school.

The figure of Mary continues to exercise its fascination. This is so not only for the devout, who themselves can profit by an enhanced understanding of their faith. It is also true for those who are simply curious, who scratch their heads in puzzlement at traditional Marian belief and piety. How is it that Catholic (and Orthodox) Christianity, otherwise regarded as typically "patriarchal" religions, can find so substantial a place in this way for the feminine—for what the Anglo-French man of letters Hilaire Belloc called in bitingly sardonic verse "a female figure with a Child"? Hopefully, this book will provide some answers.

Aidan Nichols, OP
Blackfriars, Cambridge
Memorial of our Lady of the Snows, 2013

1

The Blessed Virgin Mary in the New Testament

What is my approach in this study? I would call it the classic approach of Catholic theology, the methodology of which can be laid out in three steps—an account of which will shortly follow. I draw here on the description of theological method I offered a quarter of a century ago in my study *The Shape of Catholic Theology*, a work which has been found both representative and even helpful by those mandated to teach such theology in a wide range of institutions, especially in the United States of America.[1] So I do not think that in this "methodological introduction" I am likely to lead the reader too far astray.

---

1. Aidan Nichols, *The Shape of Catholic Theology: An Introduction to its Sources, Principles, and History* (Collegeville, MN: Liturgical Press, 1992).

A Methodological Introduction

The *first* step in classical Catholic theology—of which Mariology is a sector or department—consists in exploring the sources of revelation: namely, Scripture and tradition (on which more anon).

The *second* step consists in interrelating the fruits gained in this process, not only with each other but also with the other doctrinal convictions held by the church. Insofar as it entails relating the fruits of exploration of the sources of revelation to other aspects of Christian believing, this second step is often called "applying the "analogy of faith."" All aspects of revelation, so the principle of the analogy of faith asserts, are of their nature intrinsically interconnected. It is at this second stage that appeal to the contemporary magisterium (teaching authority) of the church is relevant, for the magisterium is concerned with the overall pattern of Christian truth, where to lose one element of doctrine is to imperil the balance of all.

Then in a *third and final* step of the classical method, the outcome of placing the fruits of exploration of the sources of revelation in a position of interrelation not only to each other but also to other key aspects of revelation is systematically reorganized by the selection of an ordering principle which the individual theologian finds especially helpful or illuminating. (Thus, for example, in the case of St. Thomas Aquinas's celebrated *Summa theologiae*, that "ordering principle" is God in the production of all creatures and the return of creation to God, which for human beings, comes about on the way of salvation.) This third step is what accounts for the plurality of theologies within the unity of a single faith.

In this systematic representation of the fruits of investigating the contents of Scripture and tradition, fruits duly contextualized by reference to the principle of the analogy of faith, the writer may well appeal additionally to philosophical concepts as aids in putting forward his or her teaching. It is a feature of a classical Catholic theological culture to hold that there is in existence a patrimony of such philosophical concepts (often called the "perennial philosophy"), an inheritance that has proved invaluable in this task. The deployment of its content by Catholic theologians helps to keep the variety of ordering principles in particular theologies within the church from becoming intellectually anarchic or from leading to a breakdown of intelligibility in a common conversation.

Before getting into the meat of Mariology itself, and bearing in mind in particular the title of this opening chapter of *There Is No Rose*—"The Blessed Virgin Mary in the New Testament"—I need to say something more about that first step in the methodology of classical Catholic theology: namely, the exploration of the sources of revelation, Scripture and tradition. Clearly, what one says about the figure that Mary of Nazareth cuts in the New Testament will be affected by the kind of approach one has to reading Scripture—or what since the nineteenth century has come to be called the "hermeneutic," the interpretative starting-point or, more widely, interpretative scheme, of this or that theologian.

The Council of Trent, in the decree on Scripture and traditions it produced during its fourth session (in 1546), describes revealed truth as found both in Scripture and in the traditions to which church life gives access in ways that are other than scriptural. Subsequently, the Second Vatican Council (1962 to 1965) in its Dogmatic Constitution on Divine Revelation (1965) emphasized the intimate unity which joins Scripture and traditions in a single global whole. A way of expressing this as a hermeneutic which would gain the support of many—probably most—classically minded Catholic theologians runs as follows. In general terms, the whole of revelation is found in Scripture, but it can only be so found when Scripture is read through the medium of the traditions—traditions which are found concretely in such "monuments" as the creeds, the historic liturgies, the teaching of the Fathers, the testimony of iconography, and the witness given to this or that truth by the devotion of the faithful.

In general, then, revelation is, as the formula has it, *totum in sacra scriptura*, "totally in sacred Scripture," which must be carefully distinguished from the Reformation principle of *sola Scriptura*, "by Scripture alone," since on this distinctively Catholic view the *totum* is not available except by reference to the traditions which are the medium through which Scripture is read, the lens we bring to reading it.

We say "in general terms" the whole of revelation is found in Scripture because even theologians concerned to stress the *totum in sacra scriptura* principle have to admit that at least two truths about Scripture are not found in Scripture itself, and these are: the list of the canonical books and the claim that all of Scripture, New Testament as well as Old, is inspired, with the various corollaries that carries. Many would add, furthermore, that "the traditions" also supplement Scripture by calling our attention to *mores Ecclesiae*, the "customs of the Church," those practical aspects of belief and worship from which theological inferences can be drawn. The latter are chiefly what, for example, the fourth-century Greek Father St. Basil the Great (for example) has in mind when he discusses this topic of the relation of tradition to Scripture.[2]

The implication of this view of Scripture, or the Scripture-tradition relationship, is that, when developing the main Mariological themes, we should aim at returning time and again to the foundational scriptural texts, but approach those texts with the aid not only of such neutral yet legitimate tools as philology, the historically precise use of

2. Basil the Great, *On the Holy Spirit*, 27.

words, but also by making reference to the traditional sources. This will mean granting authority in biblical interpretation to the exegesis of the Fathers and to the use made of biblical allusions in the liturgies and other expressions of Christian devotion whether these be textual or practical in format.

It will also mean paying due attention to the implications of the two teachings about Scripture found only in the traditions—namely canonicity and inspiration. Canonicity and inspiration tell us that the biblical books, Old and New Testament together, form, despite their diversity, an overarching unity, and that this unity is at the intellectual level a coherent, though complex, and developing truth since texts inspired by God, among whose names is *Veritas*, "Truth," cannot be in contradiction one with another.

The Primacy of St. Luke (Gospel/Acts) and St. John (Gospel/Apocalypse)

With these methodological preliminaries in place, then, we can begin to investigate the texts of the New Testament that are most crucial for the eventual emergence of the theological sub-discipline we have come to call "Mariology." The chief among these texts will already be familiar to anyone who has a decent acquaintance with the New Testament at large and the Gospels in particular. Overwhelmingly they are Lukan and Johannine, and this seems no coincidence. Why do I say that?

In the explanatory letter which prefaces his Gospel, St. Luke tells us that his own method as an historian has entailed wherever possible interrogating those who were eyewitnesses of the Word (1:2). Such concern for establishing the oral testimony of eyewitnesses was the gold standard of ancient historiography at its best. As soon as one reaches Luke's own account of the public ministry of Jesus, one finds that he names as the first four disciples of the Lord, Andrew and Simon, later called Peter, and James and John, the sons of Zebedee. These names immediately suggest themselves, therefore, as prime examples of the eyewitnesses Luke might have sought out. But we know from the Gospel of John that the evangelist, standing with Mary the mother of the Jesus at the foot of the cross, was entrusted with the care of the mother of the Lord, in a common household which ecclesiastical tradition locates at Ephesus on the Asia Minor coast.

The fact of John's intimacy with Mary together with the demands of Luke's historical method, make it likely *a priori* that the Johannine and Lukan writings have preserved the fullest Marian material and especially the fullest material about Mary derived from Mary herself. This is so even if one wishes to ascribe the final composition of the Fourth Gospel to a disciple of the evangelist, thoroughly at home with his data and imbued with his spirit. So I shall concentrate on Luke and John here, reserving discussion of other New Testament references to comment on particular Marian themes in later chapters.

The Lukan Scenes

The opening two chapters of St. Luke's Gospel, after the prefatory letter, are known to modern students as his "infancy gospel," and considerations of language as well as subject matter justify, up to a point, the separation of these sections from the rest of Luke's Gospel which this title implies. Though Luke's Gospel as a whole is clearly the work of a man who knew the Jewish Scriptures well and considered the events he was retailing to be in various ways their fulfillment, the richness of Old Testament allusion in the infancy gospel is especially thick—to take a metaphor from clotted cream.[3]

i. The Annunciation

The first Lukan episode that must detain us is the Annunciation. Luke does not spend much time setting the geographical scene—a "city of Galilee," he writes, "whose name was Nazareth" (1:26), but if we contextualize the Annunciation event in the wider stretch of his Gospel, which runs from the Annunciation via Elizabeth's conception of John the Baptist to Luke's account of the Nativity, we find that he has gone to considerable trouble in setting the chronological scene. His various indicators of the passing of time add up to seventy weeks: seventy weeks from the first appearance of Gabriel in the temple to the birth of Jesus, and this is a significant sum because in the Book of Daniel, where Gabriel makes his début in the narrative of revelation, seventy weeks is the—no doubt, symbolic—time assigned until the final deliverance of Israel (Dan. 9:24). In this charged temporal setting, then, for readers of the infancy gospel as a whole,[4] Gabriel greets Mary, a "virgin betrothed to a man whose name was Joseph" (Luke 1:27), with two words which lend themselves especially well to a study of Scripture read in the medium of tradition: *Chaire, kecharitômenê.* They are the "angelic salutation."

The usual English translation in Catholic Bibles influenced by the (Latin) Vulgate text of Scripture is "Hail, full of grace," but far from being an overly maximalist translation (as much Protestant exegesis once assumed), investigation of how the Greek Fathers and the Byzantine liturgical tradition understood those two keywords has stimulated philologists to look at them more carefully and to find their Latin (and thus English Catholic) rendering, if anything, insufficiently enthusiastic.

---

3. René Laurentin, *Structure et théologie de Luc 1–2* (Paris: Gabalda, 1957).

4. Lucien Legrand, *L'Annonce à Marie (Lc 1, 26–38): Une apocalypse aux origines de l'Evangile* (Paris: Cerf, 1981).

Whereas in secular Greek, *chaire* is a commonplace enough greeting, in those books of the Septuagint, the Bible of the Greek-speaking Alexandrian Jews, that are translated from Hebrew, *chaire* (we are told) should be translated "rejoice" or "rejoice greatly" because this word typically "refers to the joy of the people. . . at some striking act done by God for their salvation."[5] The Greek patristic tradition assumes this at all points, and the translation "rejoice" is pressed into service in multiple ways in the Akathistos Hymn, a much used lengthy liturgical poem, likely written in the sixth century.

> An angel of the highest rank was sent from
> heaven to say to the Theotokos, 'Rejoice...' He
> stood before her and began crying out:
> 'Rejoice! You by whom joy will shine forth
> Rejoice, you by whom malediction will cease!
> Rejoice, you who raise up the fallen Adam!
> Rejoice, you who dry the tears of Eve...'[6]

Three of the key instances of the Septuagint use of this verb for salvationally relevant rejoicing have it in common that they name Israel in feminine terms. Characteristically, they address her corporate person as the Daughter of Zion, a daughter who is also a mother, and they do so in the context of the fulfillment of messianic expectation. The most ancient of the three texts (the others are in Joel and Zechariah) is Zephaniah, the third chapter of whose book calls on the Daughter of Zion to rejoice, cry aloud, be glad, and be delighted, because the king of Israel is now present as "the Lord in the midst of thee" (3:15). As the rest of the angelic message will make plain, Luke sees Mary as the one in whom precisely this sort of prophecy is fulfilled, the eschatological Daughter of Zion, corporate Israel

---

5. John McHugh, *The Mother of Jesus in the New Testament* (London: Doubleday, 1975), 39.
6. *The Akathistos Hymn*, I.

8

embodied in one woman, at the climax of saving history, the happy beginning of the end of the ages.

The other key term in the opening of the angelic salutation, *kecharitômenê*, is also theologically pregnant, even more so than the Vulgate's *gratia plena*, "full of grace," would suggest. As philologists have pointed out, the verb from which this adjective is formed belongs to a family of Greek verbs all of which have the ending omicron omega, *oô*, verbs that have in common the expressing of causal action. The best translation, accordingly, is, "You who have already been transformed by grace." That is a pointer to what the Catholic dogmatic tradition will come to call the "immaculate conception." It is a point perceived in *sura* 19 of the Koran: "The angel said, "O Mary, indeed God has favoured you and made you immaculate, and chosen you from all the women of the world.'"

"The Lord is with thee" may seem, in comparison, small beer, but as the Ushaw biblical scholar John McHugh points out, in the Old Testament these words are not a conventional reassurance. Rather, they are integral to an announcement that some formidable task is about to be allotted to the person addressed. This throws light on Mary's reaction—which Luke describes as one of deep disturbance.

Since the rest of the angel's speech consists in explaining that the call of the Daughter of Zion to be Mother of the long-awaited Messiah will actually be realized in the form of what the historic creeds, taking their cue from the Prologue to St. John's Gospel, term divine "Incarnation," Mary's disturbance turns out to be well-justified. The fulfillment of the hope of Israel will take the form of a new creation in Mary's womb by the "overshadowing"—that is, the sanctifying presence—of the Holy Spirit, such that what is born of her will be not only the true king of Israel, to whom the "Lord God will give to sit on the throne of his father David," but also, and more foundationally, the "Son of the Most High" (Luke 1:32).

Whereas David's royal rank entitled his heirs to be called sons of God, according to the terms of Nathan's prophecy about the royal house in the second book of Samuel (2 Sam. 7:14), Luke reverses the order, which had run: son of David, therefore a son of God. Instead, Jesus's divine sonship will be the foundation of his entitlement to be king of Israel, and such divine sonship entails, then, for Mary, a corresponding divine motherhood. She will be, in the formula used in Byzantine iconography, *Mêtêr Theou*, "the Mother of God," or, in the language of the Greek dogmatic tradition, which achieved authoritative status at the Third Ecumenical Council, Ephesus (431), she will be the *Theotokos*, the "Bearer of God." How much did she understand of this at that point? The Flemish Dominican Edward Schillebeeckx ventures the following judgment, "In a confused but nonetheless very real way, she was conscious of the deeper implications of her motherhood—that God himself, who had once come into Israel's womb, was now to enter her womb."[7]

So far as this indeed formidable task is concerned, we can assume Luke takes it for granted that, as a woman already transformed by divine grace, Mary's mind and heart were peculiarly open to divine illumination. Nonetheless, she has very immediately one source of bewilderment, or, at least, confusion. "How can this be since I know not man?" (Luke 1:34). Another perfectly possible translation reads, "How can this be since I am not to know man." Beginning in the east with Gregory of Nyssa in the fourth century and in the west with Augustine in the fifth century, these words have been taken to imply a vow, or, as it is sometimes termed, a "proposal," of lifelong virginity on Mary's part. The discovery of the Dead Sea (Qumran) Scrolls in 1947, by filling out what was already known from such contemporary Jewish reporters as Josephus and Philo of the radical

---

7. Edward Schillebeeckx, *Mary, Mother of the Redemption. The Religious Bases of the Mystery of Mary* (London: Sheed and Ward, 1964), 27.

ascetic movement in first century Judaism styled "Essenism," has alerted modern scholars to the possibility that these patristic witnesses were on to something. The consecration of virginity to the God of Israel by a freely chosen celibate life, though a surprising development in a religion which celebrated both domesticity and fecundity so thoroughly, is a fact of the epoch of Mary of Nazareth—though there was, further back in Israel's tradition, the ancient example of the Nazarenes, people "separated to the Lord" in the Book of Numbers (6:2); Samson, in the Book of Judges, is the best known case.

It is, however, true that Mary's circumstances, as a betrothed bride, were familial and normal, not, as with the Qumran celibates, coenobitic and exceptional. Why would Mary have accepted a betrothal that of its nature would lead to marriage and hence offspring if she had in fact made a vow of this kind? For a single woman in Roman Palestine, having a husband as protector was no doubt a practical necessity if she had to leave the parental home, so a sociological argument can be brought forward here. It remains the case, though, that the content of a pre-Annunciation vow of virginity could itself only be pre-Christian, whereas the terms in which tradition has exalted Mary as *beata Virgo*, "*the* blessed Virgin," and in the words of the *Lauretana*, the Litany of Loreto, *Regina virginum,* "the Queen of Virgins," have assumed that Mary is the paradigm of a virginal renunciation of conjugal life made *out of love for the incarnate Lord.* One sees the difference. Anything less than the latter is not really Christian at all.

A solution might be advanced along the following lines. If Mary's proposal of virginity was, in her mind, a settled yet conditional one—conditional, that is to say, on what she understood of God's will for her, then with the Annunciation—when that conditional proposal became an absolute or unconditional one—it changed not only its *formal character* (from conditional to unconditional) but also its *material content* (from pre-Christian to Christian), and became an option for perpetual virginity in the exclusive service of her Son, the divine-human Messiah-king.

This will be pertinent to any account of Mary's role as helpmate of the Redeemer, or what a more daring theological usage would call the "co-redemptrix"—a theme which, as we shall see, on a *minimal* reading finds its scriptural warrant in the Annunciation episode but when treated *maximally* takes its biblical departure-point from St. John's Passion narrative, and the depiction there of Mary's standing by the cross.

The virginal conception of Jesus by Mary is sometimes seen as exclusively a Lukan (and Matthaean) theologoumenon, but apart from passing references which tell in its favor in the Gospel of Mark and the Letters of Paul, the Gospel of John speaks strongly for it—which is what we should expect if, as I suggested, John had the advantage of direct disclosures from the Mother of the Lord, disclosures shared in due course with the historian Luke. Though the testimony of St. John to the virginal conception is, by way of the famous Johannine irony, implicit in the polemical scenes of chapter 8 of his Gospel where Jesus disputes with Jewish representatives about paternity, his and theirs, an explicit assertion of the virginal nature of Mary's motherhood is found in the Johannine Prologue (John 1:1–18).

Or rather, that is so if we accept not the reading of verses 12 and 13 of the Prologue concluded to by textual scholars who have examined the manuscript tradition from the age of the great codices—the Codex Sinaiticus, the Codex Alexandrinus—onwards, but, rather, the reading presumed by *the earliest of the Fathers of the Church*. The verses, as known to, for instance, Irenaeus in Asia Minor (and subsequently, Gaul) or to Tertullian in North Africa, read:

> As many as received him, to them he gave power
> to become children of God, to those who believe
> in his Name, who was born [note the singular "was,"
> not "were"] not of blood, nor of the will of the flesh,
> nor of the will of man, but of God (John 1:12–13).

The Jesuit exegete Ignace de la Potterie stresses that in the Johannine literature as a whole, the spiritual rebirth of Christians—which copyists came to consider the exclusive subject of these verses—is never mentioned without some reference to its model in Christ the natural Son of God. He writes of the words "not of blood, nor of the will of the flesh, nor of the will of man":

> The negations are so strong, they have such an absolute characteristic about them, that it is difficult to explain them if it is purely a question of the spiritual rebirth of Christians. If, on the other hand, these negations are seen in relation to the *physical* birth of Jesus, who is born of a woman, then it is not meaningless to know how that birth took place. This negative argumentation, in our opinion, leads very expressly in favour of a singular reading of verse 13 [i. e. "who *was* born," rather than "who *were* born"]. John is arguing here with the people who have doubts about one or another aspect of the *physical* birth of Christ, notably the virginal conception (and birth) of Jesus.[8]

Where the extant Greek manuscripts *do* retain a plural—though this is concealed in English translations—is for the word put into English as "blood": "born not of blood." The word "bloods," *aimata*, is a reference to Levitical prescriptions concerning the ritual pollution involved in the shedding of blood in childbirth—primarily, through the breaking of the hymen by the firstborn. If St. John is saying here there was no such rupture of the hymen at Mary's giving birth, that is only the same as the ancient liturgies maintain when they put into poetic speech what the seventh century Lateran Synod,

---

8. Ignace de la Potterie, *Mary in the Mystery of the Covenant,* trans. Bertrand Buby (Staten Island, NY: Alba House, 1992), 106.

preparing the way for the Sixth Ecumenical Council, Constantinople III (681), went out of its way to define: Mary's virginity remained intact not only before the birth of her child but during it and after it. Mary's "virginity in giving birth"—the *virginitas in partu*—a neglected doctrine in modern theology—draws attention to the cosmic significance of this birth: how it is to change the conditions in which a fallen world exists.

I note in passing that there remains in all this the vexed question of the *adelphoi tou Jēsou*, the "brothers" (and indeed, sisters) of Jesus referred to in the Synoptic Gospels: John McHugh's well argued chapters on this topic in *The Mother of Jesus in the New Testament* conclude with a judgment which accepts while also modifying St. Jerome's influential view that "brethren" here means "cousins." After a careful investigation of the possible relations between Joseph, Mary the mother of James and Joses; and Mary "of Clopas" (that is, wife to Clopas), McHugh comes to the conclusion that the *adelphoi* were first cousins who are also foster-brothers (or, more widely, foster-siblings).

Before moving on to the great Johannine tableaux of the wedding at Cana and the passion, which have implications for, respectively, Mary as mediatrix of graces and Mary as co-redemptrix, I need to say something about the remaining Marian scenes in Luke's Gospel, the visitation and the presentation in the temple, along with the finding in the temple. I block together with these the reference to Mary's presence in the upper room, the Cenacle, in the opening chapter of Luke's other writing, the Acts of the Apostles.

ii. The Visitation

As is well-known, St. Luke's infancy gospel begins and ends in the Jerusalem temple, and, granted the identification in the Zion theology of the Hebrew Bible between the temple and the divine presence, this is already significant for construing the place of Mary, whom tradition has acclaimed in devotional texts like the Litany of Loreto as *Arca foederis,* the "Ark of the Covenant." The ark was, of course, the Holy of Holies of the desert tabernacle and the first temple, and still (one might venture to say) in the second temple, as rebuilt by Herod the Great, indicated by its absence the innermost sanctuary of the temple shrine.

There is a persuasive argument that in the visitation episode, Luke's choice of vocabulary draws biblically alert readers' attention to a comparison between, on the one hand, the pregnant Mary's journey to Elizabeth, herself still with the infant Baptist in her womb, and, on the other hand, the transfer in 2 Samuel of the ark from the fields of Kireath-jearim via the house of Obededom to its predestined home in David's capital, Jerusalem. The verb used for Elizabeth's greeting to Mary, a verb best translated "intoned," is only used in the Septuagint in connexion with liturgical ceremonies involving the ark. And just as David cried out in holy terror, "How shall the Ark of the Lord come to me?" (2 Sam. 6:9), Elizabeth in comparable awe says, "How should this befall me, that the mother of my Lord should come to me?" (Luke 1:43). The ark stayed with Obededom three months, as Mary did with Elizabeth, and Mary only reaches Jerusalem with her now newborn Son at the presentation episode, which Luke surely understands as a fulfillment of Mal. 3:1: "The Lord whom you seek will suddenly come to his temple."

iii. The Presentation

At the presentation, Mary as Daughter of Zion (it is not likely Luke will have forgotten so soon the significance of the angel's greeting *chaire*) takes Jesus to the temple there to receive Simeon's scary prophecy. The prophecy foretells that, in the course of the division the divine Messiah will cause in Israel, prompting some to rise and others to fall, a "sword will pierce your soul" (Luke 2:35). The church fathers were aware of the obscurity of these last words which are often placed in brackets in modern printed Bibles as a way of signaling how they interrupt the flow and, especially, the direction of Simeon's speech.

One suggestion is that the "you" of "your own soul" is really Israel as a whole, of which the virgin Daughter of Zion is now the representative—in which case those irritating brackets can be taken away. Since this individual, Mary, embodies the destiny of Israel and thus, in biblical terms, the hope of the world, the prophecy is fittingly addressed to her, and indeed touches her in a unique way, as devotion to our Lady as the suffering Mother, our Lady of Dolours, indicates. The wider sword and her own are closely connected in that one of her sorrows will be knowing on Calvary that the "appointed leaders of God's chosen people had refused the message of salvation."[9]

iv. The Finding

Finally, in the Lukan infancy gospel, we hear of Mary's incomprehension when Jesus at twelve years old defends his absence without leave in the temple by saying he must be *en tois tou Patros mou*, "about my Father's business," or, in an alternative translation, "in my Father's house" (Luke 2:49). The Fathers of the church do not

9. McHugh, *The Mother of Jesus*, 111.

agree in their discussion of what it was Mary failed to understand about this reply.

Probably the best solution is that she did not at this point understand that his mission was to end in sight of the temple, in his passion and resurrection, to be accomplished in Jerusalem.[10] And that is where we have our last glimpse of our Lady in Luke-Acts, within sight and hearing of the temple, in the Cenacle which is to be, at Pentecost, the place of the manifestation of the new Israel, the church. As the medieval German theologian Gerloh of Reichersberg put it, Mary is the *consummatio synagogae*, the "consummation of the synagogue." She is the image of the fulfilled synagogue and thus the image of the church—she is, in Gerloh's words, *Ecclesiae Sanctae nova inchoatio*, "the new beginning of Holy Church."[11] This is a theme which will occupy us in the seventh chapter of this book.

The Johannine Scenes

What then, in conclusion, of the two Johannine set pieces—Cana and Calvary in the Gospel of John and their coda in the Johannine Apocalypse, in the "Woman clothed with the Sun" (Revelation 12)?

i. At Cana

At Cana, when Mary intervenes with Jesus over a domestic (but, in context, deeply embarrassing) episode involving newlyweds—the failure of the wine at the marriage feast— Jesus' initial reply runs, "What, woman, is that to you and to me?" (John 2:4). The word

10. René Laurentin, *Jésus et le Temple. Mystère de Pâques et foi de Marie en Luc 1–2* (Paris: Gabalda, 1966).
11. Gerhoh, *Liber de Gloria et honore Filii hominis* 10. 1, cited in de la Potterie, *Mary in the Mystery of the Covenant*, xxxviii, n. 22.

"woman" here directs attention away from a blood relationship, which would be better expressed by the address "mother," to a different kind of relation joining Jesus and Mary. At first, Jesus defers her request rather than refuses it outright, and that for the reason given in the following sentence, "My hour has not yet come." The implication is that when his hour does come, Mary and Jesus will be in every sense united, on Calvary and in its aftermath. After that, all her requests to him will merit hearing without hesitation.

This is the interpretation given by Augustine and Aquinas, and also, it so happens, in Newman's reply to Pusey's *Eirenicon*, which was reprinted in his *Lectures on the Difficulties of Anglicans*.[12] In fact of course, though at Cana Jesus defers her request, in the sense of postponing his affirmative response, he does in the end defer to it—in the sense of accepting it, even though the resultant "sign" that he works long precedes his "hour." And so in both respects this is a little drama that looks ahead to the doctrinal thesis of Mary's mediation of graces—not least because in John's narrative, which is symbolic as well as historical, the wine into which the water is changed is the wine of salvation, the wine of life everlasting.

ii. At Calvary

This, then, is the first of Jesus's signs. The Fourth Gospel is often described as a "Book of Signs." If with various modern scholars, we count, after Cana, five others during Jesus' ministry (the walking on the water, a possible but disputed candidate, is not called a sign and by the lack of a dialogue to throw light on its meaning seems out of series),[13] then the seventh and climactic sign will be the passion and resurrection of Christ. Cana plus five other signs becomes a total of

---

12. The relevant texts are brought together in François-Marie Braun, *La Mère des fidèles. Essai de théologie johannique* (Paris/Tournai: Casterman, 1954), 56–58.

seven if we add as the seventh the glorious cross. And precisely the passion and resurrection of the Lord are the content of the "hour" referred to in the dialogue at Cana. On Calvary Mary not only stands and stands by—the starting-point of maximalist speculation on her co-redemptive role, but also, in receiving the Beloved Disciple, the archetypal disciple, as her son, she also becomes the mother of the church or, as Justin and Irenaeus will call her, the New Eve, the mother of all the supernaturally living (cf. Gen. 3:20).[14] And this will be the starting point for the doctrine of her ecclesial motherhood. Admittedly, John does not know the expression "The New Eve," nor for that matter is he familiar with its christological counterpart, the title "The New Adam." Yet it may be that he finds in Mary at the cross the embodiment of a certain little parable, with a background in the life of the first Eve, told by Jesus in his farewell discourse. This woman, Mary at the cross, is herself

> in labour, she feels sorrow, because her hour has come; but when she gives birth to the child, she no longer remembers the anguish, for joy that a man is born into the world. (John 16:21)

In what sense, though, does Mary "give birth" during the paschal mystery?

The New Testament letters and the Apocalypse frequently speak of the risen Lord as the firstborn from the dead. The birth-pangs Mary did not know at his biological birth (according to tradition, and, probably, as we have seen, the Johannine Prologue), she knew to full effect in his paschal birth, when on Good Friday she stood by his cross.

---

13. The five are: The Ruler's Son (4:46–54); The Cripple at Bethzatha (5:1–18); The Feeding of the Five Thousand (6:1–15); The Man blind from Birth (9:1–41); The Raising of Lazarus (11:1–54).
14. Idem., "Les adieux du Christ à sa mère: La maternité spirituelle de Marie dans le Nouveau Testament," *Nouvelle revue théologique* 86 (1964): 469–489.

iii. The Woman Clothed with The Sun

This is also the clue, finally, to the great drama that engulfs the woman clothed in the sun in chapter 12 of the Apocalypse, which book we can regard as, like the Johannine letters, the work of a John who used different scribal secretaries of varying literary gifts. It is a reading of the Old Testament in the light of the paschal mystery. In its starting point, chapter 12 is, as the Fribourg theologian Cardinal Charles Journet put it, "the apostolic exegesis of the Protoevangelium," the prophecy of a death-struggle between the woman and the serpent, where the offspring of the woman will triumphantly crush Satan's head (Gen. 3:15).[15] As with the figure of the Daughter of Zion, the woman clothed with the sun is an example of typically ancient Hebrew "corporate personality" thinking. This "great sign seen in heaven" (Rev. 12:1) is Israel as predestined to glory through Israel's Messiah. It is the church both as triumphant, assured of final victory, and also as still in combat on earth. Triumphant, for this is the archetypal church, fulfilling and super-fulfilling Israel, and now depicted in imagery taken from the Song of Songs "fair as the moon, bright as the sun, majestic as the marching stars' (Song of Sol. 6:9). But at the same time this is also the church "in combat," for despite the indestructibility of the church implied in her triumph, she is the object of mortal attack by the serpent, who spews out a river of lies before unleashing physical persecution.[16]

If we grant the unity of the Fourth Gospel and the Apocalypse, we can hardly mistake the Marian dimension of this "Woman." The Daughter of Zion par excellence stood by the Crucified on the great and terrible Day of the Lord. She went through torment

---

15. Charles Journet, *Esquisse du développement du dogme marial* (Paris: Alsatia, 1954), 91.
16. André Feuillet, "Le Messie et sa mère d'après le chapitre XII de l'Apocalypse," *Revue biblique* 66 (1959); 58–86, reprinted in idem., *Études johanniques* (Paris: Desclée de Brouwer, 1962), 272–310.

as she saw Jesus "born" (salvationally speaking) on Calvary (Rev. 12:2). She saw him taken up to God and his throne (12:5): literally "saw" according to the iconographic tradition which in, for instance, the ninth-century dome mosaic of Hagia Sophia at Thessaloniki, includes her with the apostles at the moment of the Ascension of the Lord.[17] (A theologian from the Orthodox East will say her presence on Olivet is no tardy invention but a given of tradition.[18]) And she was later to witness the sufferings of the "rest of her children" (12:17). But in that case the remainder of this archetypal symbol—sun-clothed, moon-girt, star-crowned—must *also* be applicable to Mary as well. It is from this text that tradition develops its scriptural understanding of Mary's assumption which, as it happens, is the only one of the six particular themes of *There Is No Rose* not mentioned in this present chapter until now. A great future lies in store for this text.

17. John Lowden, *Early Christian and Byzantine Art* (London: Phaidon Press, 1997), 195.
18. Vladimir Lossky and Leonid Ouspensky, *The Meaning of Icons* (Crestwood, NY: St. Vladimir's Press, 1982), 196.

2

The Divine Motherhood

In the context of a study of Mariology, the referent of the phrase "the divine motherhood" is presumably obvious. The phrase itself, however, used absolutely in this way, appears to be a creation of the seventeenth century when it emerges, often, as the title of Scholastic tractates on our Lady.

The Origin of the Treatise, *De divina maternitate*

High medieval Scholasticism had dealt with Marian questions incidentally, almost as an aside, in the course of exploring the being and work of the Word incarnate. By contrast, Baroque Scholasticism by a change in literary form treats Mariology as a subject in its own right.[1] Its typical perspective on the divine motherhood is to see it in terms of what we can call theological metaphysics. Such Scholastics investigated Mary's contribution to the ontological structure of the

---

1. It has been claimed that the first use of the term was in Placidus Nigido, *Summa sacrae Mariologiae* (Palermo, 1602).

act of divine incarnation, going on to treat the divine motherhood as the real explanation of all the other Marian themes that Catholic theology considers. The divine motherhood is the explanation of what they typically called Mary's privileges—the immaculate conception, the bodily assumption, and so on—though these glories also entail tasks in the soteriological order, the order of salvation: something the word "privileges" rather obscures. At any rate this is the moment in theological history that is the true beginning of modern systematic Mariology to which the twentieth-century theology of *ressourcement*—going back to the sources—was something of a counterreaction.

Criticism by *Ressourcement* Theologians

The theology of *ressourcement* was, in its Marian aspect, a reaction against early modern Mariology. Not only did it seek to bring to the treatment of Mary greater sobriety and conceptual reserve. It sought also the compensating richness of a fuller exposure to the Bible and the Fathers. *Ressourcement* theology was a reaction in the further sense that it wished to uncover a motif neglected by the first systematic Mariologists: namely, Mary's relation to the church, which *ressourcement* theologians thought of in three ways: 1) Mary's relation to the church as the church's matrix or origin (this was, we might say, a lesson about the church's past); 2) Mary's relation to the church as the church's prototypical member, the church's most exemplary member (this could be called a lesson about the church's present); and 3) Mary's relation to the church as the church's eschatological icon (a lesson about the church's future).

A Defense of the Basic Principle of Early Modern Mariology

However, relating Mary to the church cannot be an alternative to relating her to Christ—if only because the church is the church of the Word incarnate, and makes sense exclusively in relation to Christ and his mission. And for the same reason, relating Mary to the church should always be subordinate—or so I would suggest—to relating Mary to Christ, not because Mary's relation to the church is relatively unimportant but because, to the contrary, it is so important that it should be invoked in the right way, which is to say a christocentric way. Early modern Mariology was, therefore, fundamentally correct. The divine motherhood is primary and determinative, and the emphasis on it is also, so attention to the sources of revelation would suggest, fully traditional. In the last chapter I began from the Lukan annunciation narrative, which clearly implies a triune reference point for Mary's pregnancy: she has been chosen by the one who favored her with election and has already transformed her by grace. namely, the Father; she will be overshadowed by the Holy Spirit, and through the Spirit's creative and sanctifying power, what is conceived in her womb will be holy and will be called the Son of God.

Her virginal motherhood of one who is in some sense not only human but also divine is echoed not only in the Gospel of St. Matthew—whose annunciation to Joseph parallels in an obvious way St. Luke's more highly orchestrated annunciation to Mary, but also, as already mentioned, in allusions in the Gospel of St. John, especially, and, arguably, in that of St. Mark (6:3) as well as in St. Paul's letter to the Galatians (4:4). It is hardly surprising, then, that in sub-apostolic writings, as with the letters of St. Ignatius of Antioch or the *apologiae*—explanations, rather than apologies!—of St. Justin Martyr, and in the earliest of the ante-Nicene fathers like St. Irenaeus, we hear the repeated affirmation that Jesus born of the Virgin Mary is the Son of God.

Development of Doctrine and the Role of the Word, *Theotokos*

If I say that, for these witnesses, as for the New Testament writers, the sense in which Jesus was both born of a woman and nevertheless divine had still to be determined by the church, I should not be taken to mean that on this—manifestly vital—subject the church did not as yet know her own mind. The idea of the development of doctrine doesn't require us to hold that only by historical retrospect, comparing texts and sifting arguments, did the church come for the first time to a firm appreciation of revealed truth. The idea of the development of doctrine is perfectly compatible with saying that christological truth was, from the beginning, lodged in her deep mind, her profound consciousness, shaped as this was by the transforming effect of the pentecostal Spirit on her corporate response to the gospel. That transforming effect was not only moral but also cognitive, as appears from the Farewell Discourse of Jesus to the disciples in the Fourth Gospel: the Paraclete will lead them into all the truth—*them*, we notice (cf. John 14:26), not successors in ages yet to come (though the latter are also, no doubt, included). Doctrinal development consists in the articulation of the deep mind of the church, not in the progressive constitution of that mind, and for this process of articulation there is needed not primarily the archeological work of comparing ancient texts or the dialectical work of considering arguments so much as triggers or stimuli. As in, perhaps, Jungian-style depth analysis or even Proustian memory (I am thinking of Marcel Proust's great novel *In Search of Time Past*), such triggers or stimuli bring that deep consciousness to the surface.

In the case of the orthodox doctrine of Christ, the trigger or stimulus in question (it doesn't seem excessive to say) was provided above all by the word, *Theotokos*, the "God-bearer" or Mother of God. That was the word at the centre of the Christological controversy of the fifth century with its two ecumenical councils, Ephesus in 431 and Chalcedon in 451, the outcome of which was the acknowledgement of the mono-subjectivity of Jesus Christ, truly man and truly God. There are not two subjects, two Sons—Jesus, the Son of Mary, and the Word, the Son of the Father—joined by a moral bond, however unique because totally unbreakable. There is only a single Son, a single subject—hence "mono-subjectivity"—who is the actor in both divine and human activities, or, as the later of the two councils mentioned affirmed, both divine and human *natures*. The person, who in Mary's womb took human flesh, animated flesh, flesh living with a distinctively human soul and thus a human intelligence, was none other than the Father's consubstantial Word, God exactly as the Father and the Spirit are God, and consequently Mary is rightly acclaimed *Theotokos*. Nothing less—not *anthropotokos*, mother of the man assumed by the Word, nor *Christotokos*, mother of Christ, the conjunction between the man and the Word—will do.

The triumph of orthodoxy, the successful articulation of the church's deep mind, was indebted above all to St. Cyril, the principal architect of Ephesus and the chief influence, by his writings and despite the claims of partisans of St. Leo, on Chalcedon.[2] As we shall see, the theology of the divine motherhood in the writings of St. Thomas, the "common doctor" of the Catholic Church, takes the form of an increasing identification with Cyril's Christology. And yet the word "*Theotokos*" does not come from the doctors. It comes from the people.

---

2. See Patrick T. Gray, *The Defence of Chalcedon in the East* (Leiden: E. J. Brill, 1979).

St. Athanasius, the *Sub tuum,*
and "The Commemoration of Mary"

It had long been suspected that when St. Athanasius, Cyril's fourth-century predecessor in the see of Alexandria, spoke in his *Orations against the Arians* of "the Logos taking flesh of a Virgin, Mary the *Theotokos*," he was appealing to the language of popular devotion.[3] This was confirmed in 1938 when an Egyptian papyrus fragment acquired in 1917 by the John Rylands Library in Manchester was at last published and turned out to be the Greek original, dateable on technical papyrological grounds, of what had hitherto been considered a medieval Latin prayer to the Virgin, known shorthand as the *Sub tuum* (c. 250). It is a prayer which, in the common English translation, begins "We fly to thy patronage, O holy Mother of God."[4] The Latin prayer was preserved in the Western church in the Little Office of the Blessed Virgin Mary as the antiphon to the *Nunc dimittis*; used more sporadically in various devotional exercises; and was cited, in part, in the office of two Marian feasts of the older Roman liturgy: Mary, Mediatrix of all Graces, on May 31, and, significantly, the Motherhood of Mary, on October 11. The Greek original of the prayer uses the title *Theotokos* in the vocative. A literal translation of its opening words would run: "Under your mercy we take refuge, O Mother of God," and its doctrinal importance was signaled in the eighth, Marian, chapter of *Lumen Gentium*, the Dogmatic Constitution on the Church of the Second Vatican Council, which refers to it in a note in order to justify the claim of the council fathers that "from ancient times the Blessed Virgin has been venerated under the title of God-bearer."[5]

---

3. Athanasius, *Orations against the Arians* III. 29; cf. Jaroslav Pelikan, *Mary through the Ages: Her Place in the History of Culture* (New Haven, CT: Yale University Press, 1996), 59.
4. For the full text in English see, for example, *The Manual of Catholic Prayer* (London: Burns & Oates, 1962), 381.

Athanasius's letters show that by the fourth century the kind of popular devotion to which the *Sub tuum* testifies had also found expression in a liturgical setting, which Athanasius refers to in his *Letter to Epictetus* as the "commemoration of Mary."[6] In this letter, the significance of which was noted by Cyril, Athanasius argues there can be no justification for such a festival—which, according to liturgical historians, was probably a Christmastide celebration of Mary's entry into heaven, her *dies natalis*[7]—if Mary had not played a constitutive part in the history of salvation. In the *Letter to Epictetus*, Athanasius is engaging with Docetists, or what have been called Neo-Docetists—partly because of their late date (these people are teaching during and after the Arian crisis), and partly because of the special spin they gave to Docetic ideas by their assertion that the body of Christ was one substance with the Logos: in other words, that the flesh of the Lord was itself uncreated and heaven-derived. Athanasius tells them:

> You have gone further in impiety than any heresy. For if the Logos is of one essence with the body, that renders superfluous the commemoration and the function of Mary.[8]

This is a claim he reaffirms in another letter, addressed this time to a certain Maximus the Philosopher, combating what is perhaps a more sophisticated, demythologized version of the same misapprehension: namely, that the Logos became man as a necessary consequence of his own nature as the Word.[9] If Christ's humanity has always existed as a kind of component of his pre-existence as the divine Logos,

---

5. *Lumen gentium,* 46.
6. Martin Jugie, "La première fête mariale en Orient et en Occident: L'Avent primitif," *Echos d'Orient* 22 (1923): 129–152.
7. Idem., *La mort et l'assomption de la sainte Vierge. Étudehistorico-doctrinale* (Rome: Biblioteca Apostolica Vaticana, 1944), 172–212.
8. Athanasius, *Letters to Epictetus,* 4.
9. Idem., *Letters to Maximus,* 3. See on this Pelikan, *Mary through the Centuries,* 60.

says Athanasius, then the soteriological space occupied by blessed Mary would be vacant. But it cannot be vacant because the church has already acclaimed her as *Theotokos* in its worship and devotion. Athanasius argues this, be it noted, in a period when the principle *lex orandi lex credendi*—the law of praying is the law of believing—was coming to be self-consciously established. The post-Nicene fathers will refer increasingly to liturgical practice as authoritative for the understanding of doctrine, as for instance St. Basil the Great does in his treatise *On the Holy Spirit.*[10]

As already mentioned, the title *Theotokos* will be crucial for the imminent Christological debate, reminding us that a theology of the divine motherhood is situated on the cusp between Mariology and Christology, which position is entirely in order if, as I suggested at the beginning of this chapter, Mariology is itself a companion discipline of Christology and is related to ecclesiology—the only other major alternative siting—via Christology and not independently of Christology.

Nestorius and St. Cyril:
The Rejection, on Soteriological Grounds, of Dual Subjectivity

The Nestorian crisis was for the church a necessary trauma if the idea of the dual subjectivity of Christ—the "two Sons" taught by the founder of the theological school of Antioch, Diodore of Tarsus, and still found, albeit in mitigated form, in his successors Theodore of Mopsuestia and Nestorius of Constantinople—was ever to be expunged from theological consciousness. That crisis was prompted, in 428, by the dismayed reaction of monastics in the Byzantine

---

10. Bernard Capelle, "Autorité de la liturgie chez les Pères," *Recherches de théologie ancienne et médiévale* 22 (1954): 5–22.

capital to dismissive remarks by Antiochene-trained clergy about devotion to Mary as Mother of God. The title recommended by the Antiochene preachers was *Anthropotokos*, the "Mother of the man," meaning: the Mother of the man assumed by the Word at the Incarnation. But surely, the monks said, the church's word was *Theotokos*, the "Mother of God," God himself! Nestorius demurred. Strictly speaking, he said (it appears to have been one of his favorite phrases, to judge by those fragments of his writings and homilies that survive, owing to their embedding in the work of his opponents and the discovery in the early years of the twentieth century of the *Book of Heracleides*, the Syriac translation of his memoirs), Mary should be called neither *Anthropotokos* nor *Theotokos* but *Christotokos*, the "Mother of Christ." But in that case, the monks replied, parodying his chosen idiom, if Mary is not, strictly speaking, the Mother of God then her Son is not, strictly speaking, God.

In 429, Cyril's first reaction to this debate, his *Letter to the Monks of Egypt*, identified the *Theotokos* title as, to the contrary, the litmus test of orthodoxy. The singleness of the person of the Word incarnate (despite the full reality of his humanity), the mono-subjectivity of Christ which entails that Mary is the Godbearer, is a necessary condition of all belief that, in human interrelation with Jesus, we access immediately—that is, non-mediately—the creative and recreative presence and power of God, enacted, exercised, for the purposes of redemption and transformation, that is for saving and indeed, ultimately, for deifying. As Cyril typically argued in the various robust contributions he made to this debate, a differentiation of natures, human and divine, does not mean a separation of natures, still less does it mean a differentiation of subject centers.

The Orthodox patrologist John Anthony McGuckin remarks how the two constitutive ideas which recur time and again in Cyril's texts are that, firstly, "if it is not God who personally effects our salvation as the subject of the incarnation then salvation is rendered ineffectual," and secondly, and more particularly, that "a double subject Christology which divorces the man from the God in Christ makes void the Church's hope and experience of redemption in and through the Eucharist, since the Eucharist is a life-giving sacrament precisely because it is the very flesh of God himself."[11] Accordingly, the *Twelve Anathemas* or, more eirenically, "Chapters" Cyril sent to Nestorius in 430—these were propositions Nestorius was invited to condemn if he wished himself to avoid anathematization by Rome and Alexandria—open with the denial, to which an anathema was attached, that Mary was Mother of God. Though Nestorius was willing, reluctantly, under pressure and for the sake of peace, to accept at any rate verbally the *Theotokos* title, despite its lesser suitability (in his judgment) when compared with *Christotokos*, this was only on the condition that he could understand it in the distinctly Pickwickian—that is, attenuated—sense available to his own Christology. He taught that each of the incarnate Word's two natures had its own personalizing subject, but that these were joined in what he called a "*prosopon* of union," a coordinating quasi-subject. So, in Nestorius's terms, Mary would be Mother of God in the sense that she was the mother of the humanly personalized nature that was joined to a divinely personalized nature by the quasi-subject of the "*prosopon* of union," itself divine and human together. Nestorius excoriated the *Anathemas* as a whole, declaring them Apollinarian—meaning that they revived the heresy of Apollinarius of Laodicea, a contemporary of Athanasius, who had held that at the incarnation the Logos had substituted his own divine intelligence and will for human powers of mind and soul, the human powers of mind and soul that would

11. John Anthony McGuckin, *Saint Cyril of Alexandria and the Christological Controversy* (Crestwood, NY: St. Vladimir's Seminary Press, 2004), 39.

otherwise have belonged to the flesh taken in Mary. Apollinarius had been, like Cyril, a disciple of the school of Alexandria.

Let us lift a corner of the curtain that veils from us, when considering the Fathers, their setting in the world of late antiquity. The single most astute move made by Cyril's supporters was probably the shifting of the venue of the council from the capital to Ephesus. The Augusta Pulcheria, a consecrated virgin who was also the influential sister of the somewhat indecisive Emperor Theodosius II, arranged this change of plan for the general council her brother considered now to be inevitable. At Ephesus, a port city on the Aegean coast with a population of perhaps half a million, the metropolitan of the place, the chief bishop of the province of Asia and a strong Cyrilline, presided over a now Christianized city whose chief glory lay in its claim to be the final home of the Virgin and possessor of the tomb of St. John with whom she had made that home. Christian Ephesus had the Mother of God as its patroness and thus was as glorious as in its pre-Christian past when it was dedicated to the Mother Goddess, Ephesian Artemis, whose temple was among the wonders of the ancient world. Antipater of Sidon, who compiled the list of the Seven Wonders, considered the temple of Artemis at Ephesus the greatest of them all. I cannot resist quoting his description:

> I have set eyes on the wall of lofty Babylon on which is a road for chariots, and the statue of Zeus by the Alphaeus, and the hanging gardens, and the colossus of the Sun, and the huge labour of the high pyramids and the vast tomb of Mausolus; but when I saw the house of Artemis that mounted to the clouds, those other marvels lost their brilliancy, and I said, "Lo, apart from Olympia, the Sun never looked on aught so grand."[12]

---

12. For Antipater's text, see *The Greek Anthology* IX. 58.

The people of Ephesus once Christianized certainly needed a replacement, as St. John Chrysostom had led a mob to pull down the temple in 419. The building would in any case have been closed since the reign of Theodosius I, fifty years previously. Was the cult of the *Theotokos* the answer? The memory of the city's pagan ritual practices had, it seems, lingered, since the celebratory nocturnal procession with lamps with which the Ephesians greeted the council's eventual proclamation of Mary as *Theotokos* was apparently modeled on the earlier cultus. History-of-religions scholarship, with a background in learned Protestantism or anti-clerical reaction to official Catholicism, thought it discerned in popular Ephesian attitudes a certain conflation of the figures of Artemis and Mary.[13] Yet from a theological perspective, the many-breasted Lady of Ephesus, a syncretistic figure but *au fond* a fertility goddess, does not seem to have a lot in common with the Mother of the Lord. That is so, even if, as has been suggested, the breasts in question were really amber, gourd-shaped, drops, a form of breast jewelry, and not, as has also been suggested, the testicles of sacrificed bulls. The key point to emphasize in the *God-bearer* dispute is, to cite McGuckin again, the way that the word "Theotokos," was for Cyril, the "quintessential synopsis of his doctrine that the divine Word was the direct and sole subject of all the incarnate acts—including, then, that of his own birth in the flesh."[14] What happened at the incarnation was not, as Nestorius claimed, an association or conjunction, *synapheia*. It was a union, *henôsis*, and more especially a hypostatic union, *henôsis kata hypostasin*.

---

13. Theodora Jenny-Kappers, *Muttergöttin und Gottesmutter in Ephesos: Von Artemis zu Maria* (Zurich: Daimon, 1986). But Isidore of Pelusium (died 435) felt obliged to answer an enquirer who wanted to know how Christian belief in the Mother of God (*Theou Mêtêr*) related to the polytheistic belief in a "mother of the gods" (*mêtêr theôn*): Hans Belting, *Likeness and Presence: A History of the Image before the Era of Art* (Chicago: University Of Chicago Press, 1994), 32. So concern for the possible connections is not entirely a modern invention.

14. McGuckin, *Saint Cyril of Alexandria,* 154.

When we hear, as we do in the older Roman liturgy, the antiphon, "You, Mary have destroyed all the heresies in the whole world,"[15] this is what we are hearing about, and the title *Theotokos* is the necessary cipher that stands for it. The human baby Mary bore was personally hypostatized, directly and immediately, by the Word of God. The baby born from Mary after nine months of gestation was a fully formed member of the human species, but he also possessed, as his direct personal attributes, all the characteristic of deity. At the centre of Cyril's theology is the paradox of a human—and thus finite and limited as well as fragile and vulnerable—life lived out as a direct expression of God's power. As Cyril put it in his *Second Letter to Nestorius*, a text which was integrated at Ephesus with the Council's dogmatic definition, "[Jesus Christ] is said to have been born according to the flesh insofar as the Word was hypostatically united to that holy body which was born from [Mary], endowed with a rational soul."[16] And the soteriological thrust of this assertion becomes apparent when we hear Cyril add in his *Explanation of the Twelve Anathemas*, precisely on the first Anathema, authorizing the *Theotokos* title: "[The nativity at Bethlehem] was not a birth that called him into a beginning of existence but one intended to deliver us from death and corruption when he became like us."[17] So Cyril earned the acclaim the Byzantine church would give him in the troparion composed for his feast, June 9:

> Hail, translucent star,
> defending warrior of the holy Virgin,
> who shouted out above all the hierarchs at Ephesus,
> that she was the mother of God.
> Rejoice, most blessed Cyril,

15. Notably as the Tract of the Mass *Salve sancta Parens*.
16. Cyril, *Second Letter to Nestorius*, 7.
17. Idem., *Explanation of the Twelve Anathemas*, 6.

spring of theology,
and river of the knowledge of God.[18]

The Divine Motherhood in the Christology of St. Thomas

I now fast forward eight hundred years to St. Thomas Aquinas, who during his working life steadily added to his own knowledge of the Greek Fathers—partly through his close study of John Damascene's *On the Orthodox Faith*, the Christology of which has Cyril as its chief influence; partly because of the research he put into his commentary from the Fathers on the Gospels, the "Golden Chain," which used Oriental materials unearthed when writing the treatise later known as "Against the Errors of the Greeks," intended as an aid to the pope in healing the Byzantine schism; and partly because of his discovery, when teaching at the study house attached to the papal Curia at Viterbo, towards the end of the 1260s, of the full texts of the Acts of the Council of Ephesus (and the Council of Chalcedon).

The Dominican author of a work entitled, "Divine Motherhood and Incarnation. An Historical and Doctrinal Study from St. Thomas to our own Day,"[19] puts the case rather neatly when comparing the contributions of the Egyptian Fathers and Ephesus, on the one hand, and the high medieval Scholastics, including Thomas, on the other. In the fifth century, so Henri-Marie Manteau-Bonamy wrote: "The traditional cultus concerning the *Theotokos* had permitted affirmation of the truth concerning Christ. [Now, in the thirteenth century] theological precision will allow one to grasp the truth concerning the Mother of God."[20] To put that another way: what Mary contributed,

---

18. Cited in McGuckin, *Saint Cyril of Alexandria,* 243.
19. H.-M. Manteau-Bonamy, *Maternité divine et incarnation: Étude historique et doctrinale de S. Thomas à nos jours* (Paris: Vrin, 1949).
20. Ibid., 13.

devotionally and liturgically, in the age of the Fathers, to the articulation of orthodox Christology (namely, at Ephesus), she received back in the age of the medievals (notably via Thomas) in the theological articulation of her own person and role by those who had benefited from these patristic gains, bringing to the surface as they had the depth consciousness of the church.

Thomas's Approach in *The Writing on the Sentences*

Thomas's main treatments are in his *Writing on the Sentences* and the *Summa theologiae* between which a shift of emphasis has been detected—though some Thomists, such as Capreolus (the fine fifteenth-century commentator known as the *princeps thomistarum*), moved by a desire to systematize Thomas's corpus, smoothed this difference out.

Thomas's account of the divine motherhood in the Sentences commentary seems the more helpfully situated. Like the earlier Latin Scholastics, the masters of the generation before him—and unlike his own practice in the later *Summa theologiae*—Thomas in that early work approaches the Incarnation from the side of Trinitarian theology, emphasising how it would have been against the order of the divine wisdom for any Trinitarian person other than the divine Son to become human. Only one who himself has the divine nature by receiving it through generation (from the Father, i.e.) can appropriately be a son (of a human mother, i.e.) on earth.

The *Writing on the Sentences*, coming as it does from Thomas's first period as master in Paris, antedates, however, his full exposure to the Greek Fathers, and above all to Cyril and the Acts of Ephesus and Chalcedon. As a consequence, the Marian content he gives his theology of the incarnation in the *Scriptum* does not start with an account of the hypostatic union between the divine Son and humanity in Mary's womb, which is where in the *Summa theologiae*, after discussing the fittingness of the incarnation, he will begin. In the *Writing on the Sentences,* Thomas will end with the hypostatic union, but he will not begin from there. Where he starts is with Mary herself and what she furnished for the incarnation.

His perspective in the *Writing* has been called one of how something human was "prolonged" into the reality of the "eternally Engendered" divine Son.[21] In his *Sentences* book Thomas begins with the human "blood" (we would say, the human "ovum") that Mary, by her consent, offered for divine use and with the miraculous "complementation" (we would say miraculous "fertilization") of that "blood" by the Holy Spirit. In Mary, at the moment of the Annunciation, human matter in the full sense of that word came to be without the involvement of a human father, something only possible if divine action was involved.

In describing the process of human generation it is, so Thomas argues, logically correct to speak of the coming-to-be of human nature before we speak of the coming-to-be of a human person. After all, a human person is by definition a rational individual instantiating human nature: coming to be, in other words, as an instance of that nature. It was not *against* nature, then, that in the womb of Mary there was conceived, by the wonder-working power of the Holy Spirit, an example of human nature which did not yet have the concrete character of a "man," a human person. That nature was going to become ontologically complete: not, however, by human hypostatization but through its assumption by the divine Word whose personal reality will begin to terminate in it.

21. Manteau-Bonamy, *Maternité divine et incarnation,* 26.

Like the miraculous complementation of Mary's "blood," this taking up of human nature into union with the Word is the work of the Holy Spirit, one of whose names (as given him by the Latin Fathers) is *Donum,* "The Gift." It is indeed, says Thomas, a wholly gratuitous gift for an instance of human nature to be assumed into unity with a divine person. The incarnation is brought about, then, *by* the Spirit, but, writes Thomas, it is brought about *in* the Son who makes this example of human nature subsist in himself, since this unity with a divine person is to be so intimate that it will constitute total personal identity. The person of Jesus Christ is not, then, the Son of the Holy Spirit. Rather, he is the Son of the Father by eternal filiation, and the Son of the Virgin by his birth in time. The Spirit makes the Virgin fertile, and, having made her conceive the animated body, he, the Holy Spirit, lets the Son take hold of this formed example of humanity which thereafter finds itself ontologically complete since now it is a person—and more specifically, indeed amazingly, the person it now is must be acknowledged as none other than the person of the Word, the Father's eternal Son.

To the birth of Jesus, on this view, Mary made the same contribution as do all human mothers when conception takes place. If there is a difference at all it concerns her outstanding spiritual integrity when compared with all other women who have ever conceived or for that matter lived at all. Thomas asks accordingly whether Mary might be said to have merited the incarnation—to have been, so to say, its moral cause. Is this perhaps an implication of the Lukan angel's description of her as "full of grace"? Thomas's answer to his own question is negative, and yet he adds an important qualification to that negation. Once the incarnation was divinely decreed, Mary merited that it should take place specifically in her and in no other woman—deserving as much by the merit or accolade of fittingness, of *convenientia.* In terms of theological aesthetics (always involved when we hear *convenientia* language), it was altogether appropriate and remains deeply satisfying to contemplate, that the Mother of God should be the purest, most perfect woman possible—should be, in fact, Mary of Nazareth. Here, without knowing it, Thomas picks up the ending of the Greek original of the *Sub tuum* which calls Mary *hê monê hagnê, kai hê evlogêmonê,* the "sole chaste and blessed one."

From the start of his career, Thomas is, evidently, a Cyrillian in that he never lacks the doctrinal thesis of the hypostatic union. However, the scheme he presents in the *Writing* has been criticized. It sits somewhat uneasily, it has been said, with the key dogmatic assertion to which it is juxtaposed. Its logic runs: Mary's generation of the humanity of Jesus leads to the divine assumption of that humanity which in turns leads to union with the person of the Word. In the mystery of the divine motherhood, the Word thus assumes from Mary the humanity of Jesus according to what might be called a "genetic order" where parts come, at any rate logically, if not chronologically, before the whole. Consequently, Mary, a biological provider, seems in her own person extrinsic to the order of the hypostatic union properly so-called. There could, therefore, be a Thomasian theology that was more wholeheartedly Cyrilline than this one.

Thomas's Approach in the *Summa Theologiae*

The scheme just described is what is abandoned, so it is argued, in the *Summa theologiae*. In the *Summa*, Thomas no longer views the incarnation from this angle of the prolongation of the human into the eternally Engendered Word or Son. At no point in the new schema can Jesus' human conception be separated from the hypostatic union. Thomas now excludes altogether the notion that in the mystery of the incarnation a creature, i.e. the human matter conceived independently if miraculously in Mary's womb, was subsequently raised to the dignity of union with the Word. Mary did not conceive the Word *mediately*, through the way the matter taken from her was assumed divinely and thus entered into union with the Word. Rather, she conceived the Word *immediately* because in her the Word himself made human birthing his own. As the Fribourg Dominican Jean-Hervé Nicolas put it, "The mutation of the human nature in the moment of its creation in Mary's womb is not to modify it in itself but to order it to the Word as his own."[22]

Thomas's new approach entails that Mary belongs not only to the order of grace—as in her congruent meriting, as the greatest of saints, of her own status as mother of the Lord. Rather, in the scheme put forward in the *Summa theologiae* she belongs to a higher order than that of grace, she belongs to the divinely hypostatic order, the order of the communion of the Trinitarian persons. Mary's role is not now restricted to that of a superlatively virtuous woman offering biological means of entry to the divine. For the later Thomas, although the hypostasis of the Son of God has no inherent relation to the Virgin according to the Son's eternal generation from the Father, that hypostasis *does* have an inherent relation to her person through the assumption of the human nature that originates from her, in the Son's birth in time.

This affirmation will be heavy with consequences for the Mariological future. It places Mary in a different order, or as we would say demotically, a different "ballgame," from the other saints. The saints become holy—are "deified" as the Orientals say—by a gift of participation in the divine nature enjoyed in eternal communion

---

22. Jean-Hervé Nicolas, *Synthèse Dogmatique:De la Trinité à la Trinité* (Fribourg: Beauchesne, 1986), par. 317/318.

by Father, Son, and Holy Spirit. They are not, however, inherently related to a Trinitarian hypostasis. This is their difference from Mary. Significantly, in the *Summa theologiae*, as contrasted with the *Scriptum*, Thomas does not speak of Mary's dignity in terms of her merit only but in terms, rather, of what he calls the quasi-infinity God lent her dignity in making her the very Mother of God.[23] In the words of an English Dominican poet, "His [the Word's] human begetting in and birth from her/ will be protected and sustained/ by the enfolding divine Generation of the Son/ which continues in her and her Child./ This generation in her will be open/ to the Glory proper to God and limitless."[24]

For the mature Thomas, then, the divine motherhood is not a motherhood that begins humanly and is completed divinely, not even if one affirms the instantaneous character of this logically differentiable process. Instead, Mary's motherhood is throughout divine. It is a real and immediate relation to the Word in his divine subsistence, albeit in the modality of human birthing. Though her motherhood is a created relation, and one, moreover, which befalls her rather than constitutes her personal being for what it is, nevertheless it has as its immediate term the person of the Son of God. For evermore, Mary is essentially or inherently related to the divine person who subsists in the humanity formed in her womb.

A Key Proposition

If we accept the work of these two doctors, Cyril and Thomas, the most important implication of this re-situating of Mary directly within the hypostatic order runs as follows: all grace in Mary—all

23. Thomas, *Summa theologiae* Ia., q. 25, a. 6, ad iv.
24. Edward Booth, "The Annunciation to Mary: Congenerative," communication received by the present author, March 20, 2011.

sanctification and all charismata—must now be reinterpreted from the standpoint of the hypostatic order, which is to say from the vantage point of her divine motherhood as understood in a Cyrilline-Thomasian view. Expressed in a single proposition: all grace in her is either a disposition to, *or a corollary of, her state as the Mother of God: of her being the Theotokos, Deipara.*

Evidently, this is an example of the kind of high Mariology shared between Eastern Orthodoxy and Thomist Catholicism. Let us warn, however, against two conclusions sometimes drawn from it in a Western context but not, in fact, required by it.

In the first case I have in mind, which is a procedural one, Scholastic Mariologists of the Baroque and modern era sought on these principles to deduce from Mary's divine motherhood all the other elements of Marian doctrine.[25] This overlooks the fact that the mystery of Mary unfolds scripturally as a narrative on which we require to be informed, a story we need to be told for it is itself constructive of Mary's meaning in the divine plan.

The second case I am thinking of is not procedural but substantive and it lies in the maxim, *de Maria nihil satis* (we can never say enough about Mary) when interpreted to mean: Mary's belonging, alone among human persons, to the hypostatic order, gives her in right and actuality all the graces and charisms ever bestowed on any saint, however diverse the roles in salvation the missions of those saints may be. The more just conclusion is stated by Père Nicolas, a theologian already quoted. That Mary belongs to the hypostatic order means that "the personal end of this woman is the plenary and sovereign exercise of her role as the Mother of the Word incarnate."[26] All the

---

25. Mary as *Theotokos* is "the concept on which the infallible *sensus ecclesiae* has pondered, and from which all of Mary's privileges are deduced, not by frail 'arguments of convenience' but by a genuine unveiling and unfolding": thus Charles Journet, *L'Église du Verbe incarné* II (Paris: Desclée de Brouwer, 1953), 389.

graces needed for this were given her—not necessarily those needed for other tasks. Yet such were the demands of her unique role that this by itself entailed a fullness of grace God has given to no other—a proposition maintained by St. Anselm and reiterated by Blessed Pius IX in his Bull *Ineffabilis Deus* defining the immaculate conception of the Mother of God. The immaculate conception will be the first of the "dispositions and corollaries" to which we must subsequently turn.

---

26. Marie-Joseph, Nicolas, "Essai de synthèse mariale," *Maria. Études sur la sainte Vierge* I (Paris: Beauchesne, 1948), 707–741, and here at p. 718.

3

The Immaculate Conception

In the first chapter, I said that the Greek adjective, formed from a verb, by which the Lukan angel greets Mary at the Annunciation, is best translated, if we are to give the root verb its full causal force, by the paraphrase, "You who have been transformed by grace." And I suggested that this feature of St. Luke's infancy gospel was already a pointer to the immaculate conception. "A pointer." That term was deliberately a modest one. For the question at once arises, What is the character of this transformation by grace, and at what moment or moments was it arrived at?

The Impression Left by Mary on the Primitive Church

The impression left by Mary on the nascent church was a quasi-flawless one. "Quasi": that word too needs marking. The Gospels describe moments of tension or incomprehension between Mary and her Son—at the loss of Jesus in the temple in Luke, at the wedding feast at Cana in John, during the Galilaean phase of the public ministry in Mark—and these apparent "distancings," as the twentieth-century Swiss dogmatician Hans Urs von Balthasar termed them (much typical Protestant Bible interpretation would use the rougher words "rebuff" or even "rejection") raise obvious questions about the quality of Mary's discipleship. In particular, exegetes in the Greek patristic tradition found it difficult to shake off Origen of Alexandria's interpretation of the meaning of the "sword" which, in Simeon's prophecy in Luke, was to pass through Mary's soul on account of her child. Was the sword thrust, wondered Origen, a moral lapse on Mary's part, a lapse highly pertinent to faith?[1]

A number of early Greek writers, up to Cyril at least, take seriously the notion that Mary was guilty of a morally significant collapse of confidence in her Son, the climax of which collapse came on Calvary.[2] This motif of Mary's moral weakness led the Alexandrian school, of which, on exegetical issues, Origen was the master, to take a more skeptical line on Mary's moral perfection than did some Antiochenes (among others). Thus the principal historian of attitudes to the immaculate conception in the Eastern tradition, the French Assumptionist Martin Jugie, considered that on this point St. Cyril, the great champion of Mary's divine motherhood, was further away from the later defined faith of the church than was Nestorius.[3]

Effect of Cult of the Theotokos

On the other hand, the natural effect of the cult of Mary as *Theotokos* was to exalt her person simply by virtue of the excellence of her role. We saw last time how in the high medieval Latin Christian

---

1. Origen, *Homilies on Luke*, XVII.
2. Basil the Great, *Letters*, 260, 9; Cyril of Alexandria, *Commentary on the Gospel of John*, XII (on John 19:25).
3. For Jugie's work, see Vitalien Laurent, "L'oeuvre scientifique du R. P. Martin Jugie," *Revue des études byzantines* XI (1953): 7–18.

exploration of the metaphysics of the incarnation, it came to be realized by the mature Thomas Aquinas that the role of biological motherhood necessarily had implications for the character of Mary's personhood, since the immediate (non-mediate) hypostatization by the uncreated Word of the matter formed in Mary's womb carried the implication that she personally enjoyed a direct relation to a divine hypostasis, and enjoyed it moreover in the order of being—so it was not just the kind of relation other saints enjoy with the Holy Trinity at large: a relation of knowledge and love (and thus in the intentional order only).

In the terms favored by the subsequent Thomist tradition, Mary, uniquely of all human persons, inhabits the hypostatic order, the order of the Trinitarian persons themselves, and not just the order of grace—the gift of a share by knowledge and love in the divine life. A better way to put this would be to say that it is in Mary's belonging to the hypostatic order that she possesses her unique mode of inhabiting the order of grace. But then the question at once presents itself: could one so placed not be uniquely sanctified? Could she fail to have an incomparable degree of moral and spiritual perfection?

Enter the *Philotheotokoi*

In the later Greek patristic tradition we find—minus the Scholastic analysis—a cognate conviction. That Mary is the *Theotokos* implies just such an incomparable degree of holiness. The role simply must redound on the person. This is especially true of a group of writers in the seventh, eighth, and ninth centuries sometimes known as the *Philotheotokoi*, "lovers of the God-bearer."[4] The chief among them

---

4. See Francis Dvornik, "The Byzantine Church and the Immaculate Conception," in *The Dogma of the Immaculate Conception: History and Significance,* ed. Edward Dennis O'Connor (Notre Dame, IN: University of Notre Dame Press, 1958): 87–112.

were Sophronius of Jerusalem, a major actor in the controversy over the two wills of Christ which lacerated the Byzantine church in the seventh century; Andrew of Crete, much of whose liturgical poetry is still used in the Byzantine rite; Germanus of Constantinople, one of the key defenders of the images in the Iconoclast Crisis; and John Damascene, whom I mentioned in the last chapter as one of Thomas's sources and whose *On the Orthodox Faith* has been compared indeed to Thomas's *Summa theologiae* for the way it integrates so much of the antecedent materials of the patristic tradition in the service of a comprehensive overview of the Christian faith. What is especially notable about these writers—and makes them such a major point of reference in a Catholic theological apologetic, is that their concept of Mary's holiness of life is not limited to her moral performance, though, to be sure, it includes it. The moral acts Mary put in place, as a conscious agent using practical reason, so as to orient herself toward the good, are obviously relevant in an assessment of her holiness—this was why Origen considered that holiness might have been undermined by what he feared was her moral weakness—a lack of fortitude issuing in theological doubt. But the holiness of Mary, if it originates in divine transformative action, is not just a matter of moral performance, though if the action is real and corresponded with, it will be registered in moral performance as and when the demands of interaction with others require it to be. The *Philotheotokoi* make it plain in their praise of Mary that they are talking about a pre-moral or, if you prefer, a supra-moral holiness which *finds expression* in moral perfection but also preexists it, or, if (again) you prefer, coexists with it at another—higher (or deeper)—level, the level, namely, of divine energizing action affecting Mary in her bodily passions, her psychic life, and her spiritual acts.

Thus Sophronius in his *Second Homily on the Annunciation* addresses Mary by saying, "No one has been purified in advance as you have been."[5] And if we ask what point in time we are talking about in such advance purification, Andrew of Crete places it at her birth.

> The shame of sin had cast a shadow upon the splendour and charm of human nature, but when the Mother of him who is beauty itself is born, this nature recovers in her person its ancient privilege, and is fashioned according to a perfect model, truly worthy of God.[6]

In the perspective of the immaculate conception, what joins these four writers—Sophronius, Andrew, Germanus, John—is the way all hold that Mary was given preparatory graces, graces which, in the Scholastic term, "proportion" her for her unconditionally "one-off" mission of being the Mother of God. Thus Germanus in a homily on the presentation of Mary in the temple, a theme which entered the eastern liturgical tradition from the least objectionable of the apocryphal infancy gospels, the *Protevangelium of James*, takes matters back behind Mary's birth and even conception into the realm of God's eternal elective choice: "Accept her whom you have chosen, predestined and sanctified . . . , she whom you have chosen as a lily among the thorns of our unworthiness."[7] And the last of the *Philotheotokoi*, John of Damascus, puts his finger on the neuralgic point for the Western discussion of Mary's holiness, her conception in the womb of Anne from the seed of Joachim (the names her parents are given in the *Protevangelium of James*). In a homily for the birthday of Mary, Damascene apostrophizes her progenitors:

> O happy loins of Joachim, which produced a germ that is all immaculate. O wondrous womb of Anne in which an all-holy child grew and took shape.[8]

5. Sophronius, *Second Oration on the Annunciation*, 25.
6. Andrew of Crete, *First Homily on the Nativity of Blessed Mary*.
7. Germanus of Constantinople, *Homily on the Presentation of Mary in the Temple*, 8.

That the issue of just how created nature and divine transformative action were related at the moment of Mary's conception was indeed in the mind of John of Damascus becomes clear when we hear him continue, "Nature was defeated by grace and halted, trembling, not daring to take precedence over it."[9]

Byzantine homilists continued to sound this note right up until the fifteenth century when for the first time the question of Mary's immaculate conception—and not just her sanctification near or at birth, or in childhood, or during adolescence but before the Annunciation moment—came onto the agenda of the papacy via a General Council of the Church. It was easier for Greek Christian preachers to address the issue comparatively early because, unlike in the West, the Byzantine church, from the time of the *Philotheotokoi* at any rate, celebrated a feast of the conception of Anne, meaning: Anne's conception of Mary.

Compare the Latin Fathers

It was the attempt to introduce such a feast into the Latin Church—and the first clear evidence comes from Anglo-Saxon England in the decades just before the Norman Conquest—that began the eight hundred year debate on the question, resolved only, for Catholics, by the mid-nineteenth century intervention of Pius IX in the 1854 Bull proclaiming the immaculate conception as dogma, *Ineffabilis Deus*. The Latin patristic tradition paralleled the Greek, but only up to a point. As in the East, concern with Mary's status was triggered by the Trinitarian and christological controversies—Arianism and Nestorianism, but to the degree that these heresies were less widespread in the West the impact of the

8. John Damascene, *Homily on the Nativity of Blessed Mary*, 2.
9. Ibid.

post-Ephesus cult of the *Theotokos* was less profound. As if by compensation, the Latin Fathers were also less influenced by the anxieties the Greek exegetical tradition entertained on the subject of Mary's possible moral flaws (St. Hilary is an exception here). Thus, when the Irish ascetic and moralist Pelagius brought forward the example of Mary's moral perfection so as to refute Augustine's claim that, with the fall of man, no human person could escape entirely the reign of sin, Augustine had to sit up and take notice. In fact, Augustine felt obliged to make a concession to Pelagius, writing, accordingly, in his *On Nature and Grace,* "except for the holy virgin Mary about whom I do not wish any question to be raised when sin is being discussed—for whence do we know what greater grace or complete triumph over sin may have been given to her who merited to conceive and bear him who certainly was without sin,"[10] because, of course, he was the Word incarnate.

The Paulinism of the Post-Augustinian West

In the post-Augustinian West, precisely as a consequence of the Pelagian controversy with its highlighting of Paul's teaching on sin in the Letter to the Romans (cf. Rom. 5:12, "In Adam all have sinned"), there was an acute sense that in and through Adam and concretely, in practice, by descent from Adam, all human beings had contracted the stain of sin. The word for "stain" was *macula*, the contrary of which was contained in the term applied to Mary by the *Philotheotokoi, immaculata,* an exact transposition of the Greek word *achrantos.* After the fifth-century Latin Christians held that, simply by virtue of entering into human nature at biological conception, human persons take on not only a flawed moral inheritance but

10. Augustine, *On Nature and Grace* 36.42.

also a situation of originally guilty estrangement from God. This estrangement was essentially constituted by an absence of the grace life intended, in the divine creative purpose, for all human beings. It was the case even in infants who died before attaining the use of reason when for the first time they could put in place moral acts, though the inner dislocation of human powers—the loss of equilibrium which followed from the deprivation of grace—was empirically obvious only in moral disfunctionality, in moral fault. That this fundamental situation was absolutely universal—exceptionless—was underlined in another element in the Pauline corpus, Paul's First Letter to Timothy with its witness to the universal and exceptionless need for the communication of salvation by the only mediator between God and man, Jesus Christ. ("For there is one God and one Mediator between God and men, the man Christ Jesus, who gave himself as a ransom for all," [1 Tim. 2:5].) Where, then, we can ask on behalf of late patristic and early medieval Western Christians, do we hear in the praises of Mary by the *Philotheotokoi* anything at all about Mary's need to be redeemed by her Son?

Looking bifocally at the history of doctrine in the Greek East and the Latin West, we have to say it was providential that the Pelagian crisis, which left a permanent mark on the theological consciousness of the West, came when it did, so that as the high immaculist theology of the Greek church began to percolate through it was suitably challenged—as it had to be if a doctrine of Mary's immaculacy as *the mode of her redemption and not merely of her creation* was ever to be put in place.

The Arrival in the West of the East of Mary's Conception

That Mariology percolated through not in the first place by translation of the relevant writings of the *Philotheotokoi* which was comparatively late in coming but, rather, liturgically, through the reception in the West of the developed Byzantine cycle of Marian feasts.[11] Just how the feast of Mary's conception, celebrated in the East on December 9, reached such ecclesiastical Anglo-Saxon centers as Winchester, Worcester, Exeter, and Canterbury, is disputed, though the most obvious explanation is via Normandy, and, before Normandy, the Byzantine monasteries in Norman-held southern Italy. We know from an immediately post-Conquest correspondence between two black monks, Osbert of Clare, later prior of Westminster, and Anselm the Younger, abbot of Bury in Suffolk and a nephew of St. Anselm of Canterbury, that the propriety of the new feast was contested. Judged by its texts, it was a feast of Mary's sanctification, and more precisely of her sanctification either at the moment of the infusion of the rational soul into the *conceptus* or just after that moment, a moment sometimes referred to by medievals as "the second conception" (the first being the absolute beginning of the *conceptus*, at what we would term fertilization). Osbert held the object of the celebration was a transformative divine action at the moment of the first bringing into existence of the matter destined to be the vehicle and embodiment of Mary's rational soul—and therefore at her first conception or as he himself put it: *in ipsa conceptione*, in her conception in an unqualified sense.[12]

---

11. Cornelius Bouman, "The Immaculate Conception and the Liturgy," *The Dogma of the Immaculate Conception,* ed. O'Connor, 113–160.
12. For a conspectus of the unfolding of the medieval controversy see Marielle Lamy, *L'Immaculée Conception: Etapes et enjeux d'une controverse [XIIe – XVe siècles]* (Paris: Institut d'Études Augustiniennes, 2000).

Partly assisted, in the Western Middle Ages, by the rise of devotion to St. Anne, the feast of Mary's conception spread widely, radiating out from England and northern France. By 1250 it was familiar in many places, though not a few dioceses delayed its introduction till the fourteenth or even fifteenth century. These slow-coaches included the diocese of Rome where, however, the celebration was tolerated in churches owned by religious orders that favored it, notably the Benedictines, Cistercians, Carmelites, and Franciscans. The Dominicans, for reasons I'll explore in a moment, were steadfastly opposed to the Feast of the Conception, owing to the apparent theological implication, signalled both in its name and in many of its texts, that, from the first moment of her existence, Mary had no need of redemption. A well-informed Latin observer might have deemed the feast a piece of unthinking, piously over-enthusiastic Byzantine *Philotheotokoi*-ism.

Around 1400 the Dominicans accepted from the Carthusians an alternative celebration, a feast not of Mary's conception but sanctification which they kept on the same day as the Feast of the Conception elsewhere. Its collect, as found in a Dominican missal of 1504, printed at Venice, gives a good idea of what the Order of Preachers considered the true position, Mariologically speaking. The collect ran:

> O God, who after the infusion of the rational soul did
> wonderfully cleanse the most blessed Virgin Mary
> from every stain of sin by the copious gift of grace
> and afterwards confirmed her in the purity of
> holiness, grant, we beseech you, that those who
> gather in honour of her sanctification may by
> her prayers be delivered from the perils that
> assail them.[13]

13. Cited (in Latin) in Bouman, "The Immaculate Conception and the Liturgy," 145.

It was, then, a shock for the Dominicans who throughout their medieval and early modern history had been, among the various theological schools in the West, the staunchest upholders of the teaching office of the pope (they had devoted a great deal of intellectual effort to working out the various degrees of authority attaching to papal pronouncements) when by a slow but sure process the Roman Church, i.e. the church and bishop of the city of Rome, committed itself ever more fully to the innovatory Feast of the Conception (now understood as distinct from the sanctification) and its disputed theology. In 1477 Pope Sixtus IV promulgated a constitution introducing a new Proper for the Mass and Office of the *Conceptio Mariae*: the collect of the Mass used for the first time in a liturgical context the phrase *immaculata conceptio.* These texts the popes re-elaborated after the Tridentine reform. In 1708, Pope Clement XI made the feast a holy day of obligation. In 1863, nine years after the dogmatization of its underlying doctrine, Pope Pius IX reworked the festival's texts one more time, for the Breviary making lavish use of—no surprise—the homilies of the *Philotheotokoi.*

The Problem with the Underlying Doctrine

The problem with the underlying doctrine has already been indicated. As presented in its unadulterated Byzantine version it was, in a phrase of nineteenth-century Scots Presbyterians from a very different context, an assault on the "crown rights of the Redeemer."[14] It was Mariological inflation at Christ's expense. Or so it seemed. But did it have to be?[15] The general principle that the merits of Christ

14. For this controversy, see Thomas Brown, *Annals of the Disruption: Consisting chiefly of extracts from the autograph narratives of ministers who left the Scottish establishment in 1843* (Edinburgh: MacLaren and MacNiven, 1877).
15. See Charles Balić, "The Mediaeval Controversy over the Immaculate Conception up to the Death of Scotus," in *The Dogma of the Immaculate Conception,* ed. O'Connor, 161–212.

the Redeemer could be and were applied by way of anticipation to the saints of the Old Testament, to John the Baptist, and to the Virgin Mary in her life prior to the events of her Son's passion, death, and resurrection, had been taught quite explicitly by St. Anselm. Anselm's authority in Anglo-Norman England about the time of the introduction of the conception feast was considerable. His influence on medieval theological and spiritual writers was certainly profound. But the early protagonists of the feast failed to show much recognition of the important question of how Christ's anticipated merits procuring Mary's transformed existence were compatible with her *never contracting sin at all.* Among the Anglo-Norman black monk writers in England, Nicholas of St. Albans at least saw that, in his words, "the reason for the Conception is the unfathomable mystery of our redemption"[16]—which might well have led him to address the issue. Instead, he passes over it, or as the late Father Herbert McCabe used to say, "hits the nail on the side." In Nicholas's opinion feasts celebrating events in salvation history before the passion, resurrection, and ascension of Christ do not derive their holiness from the mystery of the cross but from the way that they "announce" the redemption and "adorn" it.[17]

Basically, what is happening is that the subjacent operation of a number of theological principles was impeding a more focused concern with the relation between Mary's conception and universal redemption through the cross. There was the principle of analogy, which drew into the discussion the cases of Jeremiah and John the Baptist, both of whom had been hallowed in the womb. And there was also the principle of fittingness, *convenientia,* which claimed for Mary a more radical and comprehensive sanctification than

16. Nicholas of St Albans, *Liber de celebratione conceptionis Beatae Mariae contra beatum Bernardum,* 116.
17. Balić, "The Mediaeval Controversy over the Immaculate Conception," 182.

Jeremiah's or John's. These principles conspired with two givens of the tradition: namely, Mary's eternal predestination to be Mother of God and the conviction that the goal of the incarnation was the destruction of sin and the opening of heaven's gate. These principles and givens then combined with a trio of biblical texts: the promise to Eve in Genesis 3 that in her seed she would crush the Serpent's head; the angel's greeting to Mary in the Gospel of Luke (*kecharitômenê* again); and the praise of the flawless bride of the king in the Song of Solomon, which read in the Vulgate version, *Tota pulchra es, amica mea, et macula non est in te*: "You are altogether lovely, my friend, and stain is not in you" (Song of Sol. 4:7). On this basis, high Scholastics like St. Bonaventure could grant immaculism the status of a legitimate "pious opinion." It was not, however, in their view, an opinion that ought to be preferred. As Bonaventure wrote:

> Since it pertains to Christ's surpassing dignity that he is the redeemer and saviour of all, and that he opened the door to all, and that he alone died for all, the blessed Virgin was not to be left out of this universality for fear that, while the Mother's excellence was enhanced, the Son's glory should be dimmed.[18]

The other great thirteenth-century masters agree, Thomas adding in his *Writing on the Sentences* that to contract original sin in one's own person and to be redeemed from it are correlative concepts.[19] You cannot be positively redeemed except from a negative state of affairs.

Emergence of a Desire for Compromise

Around 1300, however, there emerges what might be described as a desire for compromise between the growingly popular *pia opinio*

---

18. Bonaventure, *Commentary on the Third Book of the Sentences* at dist. 3:1, 1, 2.
19. Idem., *Commentary on the Fourth Book of the Sentences* at dist. 43:1, 4, 1, ad iii.

and the stern judgments of the masters. Henry of Ghent, the most noted of the secular masters of the early fourteenth century, grants that the fullest indication of God's love for Mary would have been to purify her from sin as soon as possible. Henry writes: "If, therefore, it was possible for her to be sanctified and cleansed from sin in such wise as to have been in sin only for an instant or moment . . . one may hold that this was the case."[20] Raymond Lull, who taught at Paris with Duns Scotus, felt that Mary's conception ought to correspond in holiness to that of her Son, but—never mentioning the redemption, which was the crucial issue—he ended his discussion rather lamely by saying no doubt the infinite power invested in the Son and the Holy Spirit could arrange it.

The Franciscan rescue of the *Pia Opinio*

The *pia opinio* was rescued for orthodox soteriology by the English or English-trained, just as it had entered the West liturgically and theologically through England in the first place. When in 1974 Father Robert Ombres and I took the French Dominican Yves Congar to lunch at Trinity College, Cambridge, as the guest of the Dean, J. A. T. Robinson of *Honest to God* fame, and an *enfant terrible* in both exegesis and theology, Robinson told us he had been reading the Christology of Thomas Aquinas. "Dreadful stuff," he said, "almost Docetic," the "result of Alexandrian influence, of course," and how his depression had been lightened by the discovery that Aquinas had denied the immaculate conception. But, said Congar, struggling to find a formula for politeness, "It is the gift of your England to the catholicity." I shall forebear to repeat John Robinson's response but the English or English-trained Franciscans William of Ware and

20. Balić, "The Mediaeval Controversy over the Immaculate Conception," 198.

Blessed John Duns Scotus certainly opened up the soteriological exit from a devotional impasse. William provided a trigger when he wrote that Mary needed the Passion of Christ on account of that which *would* have been in her *had her Son not preserved her*. And Scotus responded by developing a distinction between the preservative and reparatory application of Christ's merits, the distinction which would eventually be canonized in Pius IX's bull. In Scotus's last work, the *Ordinatio*, written in his own hand and still unfinished at his death, he gives the fullest account of argumentation already laid out in the various versions of the *Reportationes*: notes on his lectures in Paris and Oxford. Was Mary incapable of undergoing a divine act in the first moment of her existence? No: God could give her, should he wish, as much grace then as he does to other pre-moral souls at infant baptism or, under the Torah, at circumcision. Could this have been in the first moment of the existence of the *conceptus*, though? Why not? There is nothing absurd about a soul being created, united with the flesh, and adorned with grace, all in the same instant. But wasn't she by nature a daughter of Adam, which would make her—by definition—lacking in original justice? Scotus replies, nature is just as much prior to the privation of justice as it is to justice itself. As to nature, all that can be stated is that it pertains to nature to be the foundation of Adamic filiation—to being a son or daughter of Adam. Neither justice nor the lack of it is included in the concept of nature thus considered. Lastly, there comes the "sixty-four thousand dollar" question: Is not redemption universal? Scotus writes, "Just as others are in need of Christ for the remission, by his merits, of the sin they have already contracted, so Mary would have been in still greater need of a Mediator preventing her from contracting sin."[21] As a coda, Scotus adds for good measure: If Christ is a perfect redeemer

21. Cited ibid., 207.

he should have saved at least one person from contracting original sin: the richness of his redemption is augmented, not diminished, if it is exercised in both the preservative and the reparatory modes.[22]

The almost immediate rallying to the Scotist theology of the immaculate conception, which now became the *nova opinio*, the increasingly predominant albeit new opinion (rather than simply *pia opinio*) suggests it was the way forward the *sensus fidelium* was instinctively looking for—a way forward at the reflective or, as the Rahnerians say, "thematized," level of theological thought. In 1438, the Council of Basle—albeit in its non-ecumenical phase since the papal legates had just withdrawn—defined Mary's immaculate conception "by a special effect of divine preventing [i.e. prevenient] and operating [i.e. operative] grace."[23] In large parts of Europe, especially north of the Alps and in the Iberian Peninsula, this was considered an authoritative synodical decree. The iconography of the immaculate conception now becomes more or less standardized in church art in the West—the Virgin placed centrally, standing on cloud, surrounded by symbols drawn from Scripture—the garden enclosed, the tower of David, the unblemished mirror, the sealed fountain, the gate of heaven, the lily among thorns, while God looks down on her as the perfect realization of his tender love for man.[24] In the years 1482/1483 Pope Sixtus IV declared it wrong to say the Roman Church celebrates only Mary's post-conception sanctification in the womb. From 1497 all candidates for theological degrees at the Sorbonne had to take an oath to defend the new doctrine. And by

22. But see Gabriele Maria Roschini, *Duns Scoto e l'Immaculata* (Rome: Centro di Studi Francescani Liguri, 1955) whose thesis it is that Scotus moved from regarding the theologoumenon as possible (when teaching at Oxford) to probable (when teaching at Paris).

23. Cited in Wenceslaus Sebastian, "The Controversy over the Immaculate Conception from after Scotus to the End of the Eighteenth Century," in *The Dogma of the Immaculate Conception,* ed. O'Connor, 232.

24. Maurice Vloberg, "The Iconography of the Immaculate Conception" in *The Dogma of the Immaculate Conception,* ed. O'Connor, 463–512.

1700 some 150 universities had followed suit. Among the religious orders, the Society of Jesus officially adopted the doctrine in 1593. Throughout the sixteenth and seventeenth centuries and for much of the eighteenth, the Spanish crown regularly petitioned the papacy for a final and definitive declaration of its truth. In Spain, *la Purissima* was the national patron.

Dominican Difficulties

The major Dominican theologians of the post-Tridentine epoch, with some few significant exceptions, refused to yield, even though in other quarters theologians had moved on to discussing the definability of what was a well-nigh universally recognized truth of faith among those in Catholic communion. The German Dominican Ulrich Horst of the Martin Grabmann Institute in Munich explains why. His 1987 study, "The Discussion about the Immaculate Conception in the Dominican Order" bears the instructive subtitle, "A Contribution to the History of Theological Method."[25] The difficulty they saw was not only soteriological—though Dominican theologians did not necessarily accept Scotus had completely resolved that issue. Nor was it simply a matter of fidelity to the teaching of St. Thomas, though in the early 1850s Pius IX had to assure some delicate consciences that if there were friars who felt their oath to uphold Thomas's teaching prevented them from celebrating the feast, the pope would be happy to release them from the promise they had made. Shortly after this, incidentally, the Holy See invited the Dominican master general to have the word *immaculata* added before *conceptio* in the order's liturgical books in preparation for the dogmatization of the doctrine shortly expected. But as Horst

25. Ulrich Horst, *Die Diskussion um die Immaculata Conceptio im Dominikanerorden: Ein Beitrag zur Geschichte der theologischen Methode* (Paderborn, Germany: F. Schöningh, 1987)

shows, the great stumbling-block in the early modern period was theological method. To accept the *nova opinio* as well-founded was in effect to say, so the Dominicans objected, that in theological method the *sensus fidelium* and the liturgical practice of the church could count as weightier than the combination of the literal sense of Scripture, the patristic consensus, and the common doctrine of the high medieval divines. The vulgar crowd, the *novi doctores* and the alteration of the calendar could trump these other authorities. As Horst reports, the Dominicans had failed to develop a positive concept of the *sensus fidelium*. The chief theologian of the Society of Jesus, Francisco Suárez, could have told them that the "sense of the faithful," in Horst's paraphrase, "does not constitute the truth of faith but exercises a hermeneutical function on account of the defective unequivocalness of the sources" (i.e. Scripture and tradition),[26] and thus, in a centuries-long process, creates the clarity that enables the highest teaching office to deliver a definitive judgment. So in the wider church, things had progressed beyond the state of affairs when at the early sixteenth century Fifth Lateran Council, Cardinal Cajetan, the Dominican Thomas de Vio, was asked by Leo XI to advise him, whether to sanction the doctrine finally or not. Cajetan replied the pope must choose between, on the one hand, Scripture and the Fathers, and, on the other, the faithful and the liturgy.

Cajetan's Solution

Even if this reply may have been, as some think, ironic, it was the same Cajetan who, more usefully on a long overview, removed the lingering Dominican—or perhaps one should say Thomist—doubts about the soteriology involved. *Pace* Scotus, redemption, even

---

26. Ibid., 101: "wegen der fehlenden Eindeutigkeit der Quellen."

preservative redemption, must be in some sense redemption from, as well as redemption for. Scotus had not said what Mary's grace of original righteousness was redemption from. It was, taught Cajetan, from non-orderedness to grace. Mary though she might be unstained was nevertheless, in the perspective of engracement, "in debt." Pius IX, defining she was indeed unstained, left untouched the question of that debt or non-orderedness to grace which is the fulcrum on which a Neo-Thomist theology of the immaculate conception can turn. Newman, writing to Pusey in 1866, and seeking to meet the Tractarian leader's objections to the dogma made full use of Cajetan's contribution.

> [W]e consider that in Adam she died, as others, that she was included, together with the whole race, in Adam's sentence; that she incurred his debt, as we do; but that, for the sake of Him who was to redeem her and us upon the Cross, to her the debt was remitted by anticipation, on her the sentence was not carried out . . . Mary could not merit . . . the restoration of that grace, but it was restored to her by God's free bounty, from the very first moment of her existence.[27]

The twentieth-century Toulouse Thomist Marie-Joseph Nicolas would put the same teaching in terms of non-orderedness rather than the—to some, off-puttingly—penal-sounding language of the "debt":

> It is certain that grace presupposes the nature which receives it. In that first instant of a nature, prior to the instant in which grace is possible, there is neither grace nor privation of grace, but only a natural ordination not to have grace [i.e. non-orderedness to grace]. This is what Mary contracted, and from which she is saved.[28]

In conclusion: all Catholic theologians, or all orthodox Catholic theologians, would agree that the formal raison d'être of the

---

27. John Henry Newman, *Certain Difficulties felt by Anglicans in Catholic Teaching Considered* (London: Longmans, Green, 1907), II.48.
28. Marie-Joseph Nicolas, "The Meaning of the Immaculate Conception in the Perspective of St Thomas," in *The Dogma of the Immaculate Conception*, ed. O'Connor, 334.

immaculate conception is Mary's predestination to the divine motherhood. It is a means for which her condition as *Theotokos* calls. What is more disputed is what I shall consider next: the claim that the predominant theological outcome of the definition of the immaculate conception should be concern for Mary's co-redemptive role. What are the implications of that strange ambiguity of pronouns (as between Hebrew, Greek, and Latin) in the proto-gospel, Genesis 3:15? Is it a "he" or a "she" who crushes the serpent's head, or is it in some sense both he and she (the "Christo-Marian" reading, for which the "seed" is Christ but "the woman" Mary)?[29] How is the raison d'être of the immaculate conception affected if we say that the incarnation to which the immaculate conception is ordered is essentially a redemptive incarnation? After all, it was for the sake of his redemptive entry into the world that the Logos created in Mary the fully redeemed presupposition for that entry. Mary was not meant to be, in Edward Schillebeeckx's words, "a kind of 'extra-Christian' child of Paradise."[30] To the contrary, her immaculate conception was so that she might "take part in the victorious struggle of the Only-begotten Son with the Enemy."[31] As the German Jesuit theologian Karl Rahner pointed out, she is "the one redeemed person without whom the redemption qua victorious cannot be thought."[32] If so, what was the Immaculate doing at the cross? Obviously, if Marian co-redemption is an implicate of the immaculate conception, and Marian co-redemption is a thesis that remains undogmatized and

---

29. René Laurentin, "L'interprétation de Genèse III.15 dans la Tradition jusqu'au début du XIIIe siècle," *Études mariales* 12 (1954): 79–156.
30. Schillebeeckx, *Mary Mother of the Redemption*, 69.
31. C. de Koninck, "The Immaculate Conception and the Divine Motherhood, Assumption and Coredemption," in *The Dogma of the Immaculate Conception*, ed. O'Connor, 363–412, and here at 365.
32. Karl Rahner, "Die unbfleckte Empfängnis," in idem., *Schriften zur Theologie* (Einsiedeln: Benziger, 1954), 236.

indeed contested by many Catholic theologians, the doctrinal story of the immaculate conception is unfinished after all.

4

The Co-redemptrix

I mentioned in my opening chapter, à propos of Mary's standing by the cross in the Gospel according to St. John, that theologies of Marian co-redemption come in two varieties: which we can term "minimalist' and "maximalist." The first kind, the minimalist one, which, leaving aside the disputed question of the *word* "co-redemptrix," is non-controversial, locates Mary's contribution to the redemption in her response to Gabriel at the Annunciation—drawing, then, for its scriptural basis on the Lucan infancy gospel (Luke 1:26–38). The second kind of theology of co-redemption, the maximalist version, is the trickier one. While not denying—rather, affirming—the co-redemptive significance of the Annunciation event, it ties the co-redemption climactically if not indeed essentially to Mary's role in the drama of the cross—as portrayed in the Johannine passion narrative (John 19:25–27).

"Subjective" and "Objective" Theologies of Co-redemption

As we shall see, accounts of Mary's contribution to the Atonement, and not simply to the incarnation, themselves fall into two main sorts, which can broadly be described as, respectively, objective and subjective in character. The *subjective* co-redemption-at-the-cross theme is closely linked to the topic of Mary's role as dispenser of grace—itself more thoroughly attested in tradition, in both the Western and Eastern streams, though not for that reason more acceptable, necessarily, to classical Protestants. Subjective co-redemption can also be synthesized with the topic, more popular in our own day, of Mary and the church. On the subjective understanding of Mary's contribution to the atonement, that contribution is restricted to a role in the transmission of the fruits of Christ's sacrifice—whether that transmission be thought of as an exercise carried out within the heavenly communion of saints or by means of the earthly (yet certainly not for that reason purely natural) organism of the church, whose archetype the Virgin Mother is.

By contrast, for the *objective* theology of Marian co-redemption, our Lady's role is not restricted to such transmission of the gains of the atonement to other human subjects (which is the sense of the word "subjective" in this context). Instead, her contribution enters into the overall constitution of Christ's sacrifice as that sacrifice transpired in itself before God. This is a claim which, even in the Mariologically highly charged atmosphere of the 1940s and 50s, elicited no general consensus among Catholic theologians. Coming to a conclusion about it—broadly speaking, in its favor—will be the purpose of the present chapter.

I said that the distinction between a minimalizing and a maximalizing theology of the co-redemption turns, however, not mainly on this difference (subjective or objective?), because even a subjective theology of co-redemption, such as I just flagged up, is maximalizing when seen in an ecumenical context—as also, perhaps, when regarded against the background of the median or average Catholic theological consciousness in the post-conciliar epoch. To repeat: the distinction between a minimalizing and a maximalizing theology of the co-redemption turns principally on whether the co-redemption is linked to the Annunciation exclusively or to both the Annunciation and the cross.

The Relation of the Incarnation to the Passion

Much of the patristic material that has been adduced in favor of a maximalizing theology of co-redemption is, it must be confessed, ambiguous insofar as it is difficult to decide whether the writers concerned have the intention of pressing their case beyond the circumstances of Christ's conception and birth to those of his passion and death as well. This is not a problem merely for those with Mariological questions to bring to the Fathers. It is a problem for patristic soteriology more widely. What do the Fathers mean when they describe the incarnation as a *redemptive* incarnation? Do they mean, firstly, redemptive in and of itself, irrespective of the Lord's sacrificial death which was de facto its outcome? Or do they mean, secondly, redemptive insofar as, logically speaking, the incarnation was a necessary condition of that death, for clearly there could be no one to die on the cross unless that someone had first been born? Or do they mean thirdly and finally, that the incarnation was redemptive inasmuch as it was ordered, always and intrinsically, to the paschal mystery, so that all statements assigning redemptive value to the events of the incarnation—including, then, statements assigning co-redemptive value to acts contributing to the incarnation—require interpreting "staurologically," that is, by reference to the cross?

Patristic Texts Relevant to Co-redemption

Basically, so far as Marian co-redemption is concerned, in the patristic period we are dealing with a small number of texts that patently regard the redemptively collaborative role of Mary at the Annunciation as recreated at the foot of the cross, and a larger number of texts where such a projection forward of her Annunciation role to a similar role at the atonement is a matter of the speculative interpretation of later theologians—though we should note that the word "speculative" should not be taken to signify "ill-founded," much less *un*founded or untrue. If among my trio of possibilities for how to take patristic talk of a redemptive incarnation we are inclined to select the third—for which the incarnation event is only redemptive when seen as intrinsically ordered to the cross—we might in that case be inclined to give ambiguous testimonies to a maximalist theology of Marian co-redemption the benefit of the doubt.

Thus the French Jesuit Bertrand de Margerie, a scholar who was equally at home in biblical studies and the world of the Fathers, in an essay on "Marian Co-redemption in the Light of Patristics," is willing to press into the service of co-redemptive maximalism a number of just such ambiguous texts from the sub-apostolic period—for instance, from Ignatius of Antioch and Melito of Sardis. So, for example, when in his Letter to the Ephesians Ignatius writes: "The prince of this world ignored the virginity of Mary, her childbirth, and the death of the Lord, three resounding mysteries that were accomplished in the silence of God,"[1] de Margerie interprets as follows:

> The dying Lord, acting in the silence of the Father, is the Son who caused the virginity of Mary. The resounding mystery . . . of the virginal

1. Ignatius, *Ad Ephesos* 19, 1.

motherhood of Mary, seems to be not only a condition, willed by the Father and the Son, of the saving death of the Lord on the Cross, but also a free co-operation with it, and even a privileged and unique co-operation in his redeeming death.[2]

One would hardly draw this large inference from Ignatius's laconic text unless one held that the incarnation is always and in all respects ordered to the cross.

Similarly, when in his *On the Pasch* Melito calls Christ "the voiceless Lamb, the Lamb who was slain, born of Mary, the kind ewe lamb . . . he it was who rose from the dead and raised man from the depths of the grave,"[3] de Margerie comments, "[B]y qualifying Mary as the ewe lamb, Melito signifies her participation in the sacrifice of the Lamb of God"—a statement that finds some support from the editor of the *Sources Chrétiennes* edition of Melito's *On the Pasch* when he remarks that in calling Mary the ewe lamb Melito inevitably summoned up the idea not only of purity but also of sacrifice.[4] Melito probably had in mind Old Testament texts from Leviticus and the Book of Numbers about a ewe lamb sacrificially offered.[5]

From patristic texts which, partly owing to their brevity, are hardly self-interpreting, to say the least, we can move on to the smaller constituency where something akin to the later doctrine of Mary's co-redemptive role at the cross is unambiguously in mind. The best example is a passage from St. Ambrose's commentary on the Gospel of Luke which the fourth-century doctor was evidently pleased with because he reproduces it virtually in its entirety in his letter to the church of Vercelli.[6]

---

2. Bertrand de Margerie, "Mary Coredemptrix in the Light of Patristics," in *Mary. Co-redemptrix, Mediatrix, Advocate: Theological Foundations,* ed. Mark Miravalle (Santa Barbara, CA: Queenship, 1995), 5.

3. Melito, *De Pascha* 71. 11. 513–520.

4. Othmar Perler (ed.), *Méliton de Sardes. Sur la Pâque et fragments* (Cerf: Paris, 1966 = *Sources Chrétiennes* 123): 176.

5. Lev. 5:6 and Num. 6:14; 7:17

His mother was there also, the zeal of her charity making her scorn the danger. . . . While the apostles were in flight, she stood before the Cross, animated by sentiments worthy of the Mother of Christ. She contemplated with love the wounds of her Son, for she was less preoccupied with the death of her child than with the salvation of the world. Perhaps indeed, knowing that by the death of her Son the redemption of the world was worked, she hoped to be able by her own death-to-herself to contribute some little to what was accomplished for the profit of all.[7]

That final (albeit tentative) statement lacks the precision of later theology but it can hardly be denied that it constitutes an example of what I am calling the maximalist objective view.

Between the ambivalent and rather cryptic (because over-brief) comments of Ignatius and Melito, and Ambrose's fairly fully-fledged and clear account comes, both chronologically and theologically, the work of St. Irenaeus who represents an intermediate line of thinking which will eventually be of great importance for the co-redemption theme, and that is the doctrine of Mary as the New Eve. The parallelism between Eve and Mary which this doctrine posits runs as follows: by investigating the role of Eve at our creation and fall we can work out the role of Mary at our recreation and rehabilitation. St. Paul's account of Christ as the New Adam, reestablishing humanity in grace by his saving action, did not explicitly speak of a New Eve—this is the lacuna Irenaeus fills,[8] anticipated by Justin and followed by innumerable later Fathers, shapers of the ancient liturgies and the subsequent doctors.[9] St. Paul's comparison between the old Adam and the New Adam, in having recourse to the Book of Genesis so as to throw light on the nature

6. Ambrose, *Epistolae* 63, 109–110.
7. Idem., *Expositio evangelii secundum Lucam* X. 132.
8. Irenaeus, *Adversus haereses* III. 22, 4; V. 19. 1–2; Ibid., *Demonstratio apostolicae praedicationis* 33.
9. Lino Cignelli, *Maria nuova Eva nella patristica greca, sec. II–IV* (Assisi: Porziuncola Edizioni, 1966).

of Christ's saving work, implicitly contained a further comparison: one, namely, between the first and the Second Eve. The plan of redemption, as announced in the Genesis "protevangelium," Gen. 3:15, had appealed to "the Woman" as a continuingly relevant figure in the salvation history that was to unfold. That is what John Henry Newman in his response to the *Eirenicon* of the Tractarian divine E. B. Pusey called "the great rudimental teaching of Antiquity from its earliest date concerning [Mary]." Newman explained: "[I] mean the *primâ facie* view of her person and office, the broad outline laid down of her, the aspect under which she comes to us, in the writings of the Fathers. She is the Second Eve." [10]

And when Newman goes on to "consider what this implies," what he comes up with is a version of the principle I have already given you. In his words, "We are able, by the position and office of Eve in our fall to determine the position and office of Mary in our restoration." [11] The way in which the doctrine of the Second Eve continued to structure the mid-twentieth century theology of Marian co-redemption can be seen from an English Catholic study of 1938, a second edition of which was published in 1954. In Canon George Smith's *Mary's Part in our Redemption* we read:

> In the earliest Christian writers we do not find Mary's redemptive function worked out in all its consequences and implications; nor even today have theologians finished the work of elucidation. But essentially the whole doctrine of Mary's part in our Redemption is contained implicitly in the statement that, as Christ is the Second Adam, so Mary is the Second Eve. [12]

---

10. Newman, *Certain Difficulties Felt by Anglicans*, II, 32.

11. Ibid., 32; cf. Marie-Martin Olive, "Un petit traité de mariologie selon les Pères des premiers siècles: La Lettre à Pusey de Newman (1865)," in *Primordia cultus mariani* III (Lisbon, 1967), 303–332, and, more widely, Hubert du Manoir, "Marie, nouvelle Eve, dans l'oeuvre de Newman," *Études mariales* 14 (1956): 67–90.

12. George D. Smith, *Mary's Part in Our Redemption,* 2nd ed. (London: Burns and Oates, 1955), 42.

The Medieval Development

Before we explore the magisterial teaching pertinent to this, and then the dogmatics concerned, I ought to mention the medieval development. Against a background where the primary sense of Mary's co-redemptive role remained the Annunciation, as in St. Bernard and St. Thomas, that development consists in the emergence of the motif of the compassion of the Mother of the Lord—"compassion," not chiefly in the sense of the quality of mercy but in the etymologically more original sense of *co-passio*: Mary's "suffering-with" her divine-human Son. As we shall see, the word increasingly used was *transfixio*, in effect a spiritual crucifixion undergone by Mary on Calvary in her role as companion of her Son.[13] Carolingian writers had already created a Marian category of "super-martyrdom." At the cross, we read in a letter transmitted in Jerome's corpus but ascribed by modern scholarship, at any rate tentatively, to Paschasius Radbert, monk of Corbie in northern France, she was *plus quam martyr*, "more than a martyr."[14] "More than a martyr" is a phrase that seems obviously related to the notion of Mary's "transfixion" at the crucifixion, a notion that dominates the texts for the Lenten feast of our Lady "of the Seven Sorrows" which gradually made its way into medieval calendars. And just as the white monks, the Cistercians, readily adopted the initially black monk, Benedictine, theology of Mary's immaculate conception, so here too (accepting that is, the Paschasian origin of Pseudo-Jerome's letter) we find hints of a theology of Marian transfixion in St. Bernard, notably in the so-called "Sermon of the Twelve Stars."[15] This teaching

---

13. Jean Dissard, "La transfixion de Notre Dame," *Études* 155 (1918): 257–286. The periphrastic phrase "spiritual crucifixion" was used by Pope John Paul II during his visit to the Marian shrine of Alborado, at Guayaquil, Ecuador, on January 31, 1985: see *Osservatore romano* (English language edition), No. 876, for March 11, 1985, 7.
14. Pseudo-Jerome (Paschasius Radbert), *Epistola "Cogitis me."*

becomes fully explicit in Bernard's biographer and friend Arnold of Bonneval—on whose doctrine something more, therefore, should be said.

In his tractate *On the Seven Words of the Lord on the Cross,* Arnold first presents a densely symbolic theology of the co-redemption based on typology.[16] He draws a comparison between, on the one hand, the two altars of the Old Law, the altar of incense at the entrance to the tabernacle, the Tent of Meeting, and the altar of holocaust in front of the Holy of Holies, and, on the other hand, what he calls the two altars of the New Law, the altar of the heart of Mary where the soul of Christ was sacrificed and the altar of the body of Christ where the Lord was sacrificed in his own flesh. But this way of putting things obviously threatens to compromise the unity of the redemptive act. Accordingly, Arnold paused, remembering perhaps the warning given by St. Ambrose in his commentary on Luke—cited almost literally in another of Arnold's writings, the *libellus* or "little book" on "The Praises of the Blessed Virgin Mary"—that the sacerdotal prerogative belongs to Christ alone.[17] And so Arnold proceeds to restate his teaching about Mary's stance on Calvary, producing a more careful and less imaginative formula which reads as follows: "the love of the Mother co-operated greatly in its own order to make God propitious to us, since the charity of Christ presented to the Father [both] his own vows, *vota*, and those of his Mother."[18] (The term *vota* here means "intention"—a single but complex intention, we can say, since its object was the glorification of God by the redemption of man, a glorification by redemption which

15. Bernard, *Sermo in signum magnum* 14–15. See H. Barré, "S. Bernard, docteur marial," in Auctores varii, *S. Bernard théologien* (Rome, 1953, = *Annales S. O. Cist.,* 9), 92–113.
16. Arnold of Bonneval (also called Arnold of Chartres), *Tractatus de septibus verbis Domini in cruce,* 3.
17. Idem., *De laudibus beatae Mariae Virginis.*
18. Idem., *Tractatus de septibus verbis Domini in cruce,* 3.

brought to completion the plan of salvation.) Summing that up in a two-word Latin tag, Arnold declares that Mary "was co-crucified by love," *concrucifigebatur affectu*, thus factoring in something like the ninth-century Paschasian "super-martyr" idea.[19]

Finally, where the Middle Ages are concerned, the comprehensive Mariological *Summa* long attributed to St. Albert the Great, the highly influential *Mariale* of the Pseudo-Albert,[20] speaks of Mary in a phrase that will enter papal magisterial teaching as well as the Roman liturgical tradition when it calls her *adiutrix Redemptoris*, the "helpmate of the Redeemer," an echo of Gen. 2:18 where the Lord God proposes to make for Adam "a helper fit for him." That would come into the category, then, of New Eve theology. As the *Mariale* puts it, "As Eve was the occasion for Adam of his loss, so [in, we can say, a recapitulation that reverses the outcome of the fall] Mary was the occasion for Christ of aid in his redeeming work."[21] The *Mariale* understands Mary's compassion—by this date a given of Marian devotion in the West (one thinks of the thirteenth-century sequence, the *Stabat mater*, still used in the modern Roman liturgy[22])—as her cooperation in Christ's redeeming intention. As "consort of the Passion," *consors passionis*, she became the "mother

19. Intriguingly, a similar vacillation to Arnold's on whether or not it is appropriate to describe Mary's role on Calvary in sacerdotal terms—Arnold's co-nationals in the seventeenth-century French school had thought it was—is apparent in shifting attitudes on the part of the Holy See in the early twentieth century. Whereas in 1906 Pius X approved and attached indulgences to a prayer seeking Mary's intercession as the "Virgin Priest," in 1916 the Holy Office forbade the iconographic depiction of Mary in the vestments of a priest—a "priest," evidently, engaged in offering her Son. See the entry "Priesthood of Mary, Priests and Mary" in Michael O'Carroll, *Theotokos: A Theological Encyclopaedia of the Blessed Virgin Mary* (Collegeville, MN: Liturgical Press, 1982), 293–296.

20. The author was probably a German Dominican in Albert's circle; see the comments of T. R. Heath, incorporated in St. Thomas Aquinas, *Summa Theologiae, Volume 51. Our Lady* (London: Eyre and Spotiswoode, 1969), 86.

21. Pseudo-Albert, *Mariale*, q. 29, a. iii.

22. See on this Sandro Sticca, *The "Planctus Mariae" in the Dramatic Tradition of the Middle Ages* (Athens, GA: University of Georgia Press, 1988).

of the regeneration," *mater regenerationis*. The author of the *Mariale* holds that at the cross, as at the Annunciation, Mary represented all humanity for whom the sacrifice of her Son was being offered. Continuing a venerable comparison with what happens at the eucharistic liturgy, the comparison Ambrose had initiated and Arnold of Bonneval resumed, the Pseudo-Albert proposed that, standing at Christ's side, Mary does everything that is required at Mass of the faithful Christian when he or she offers the saving Sacrifice, renewed sacramentally at the altar, through and with the ministerial priest. When the Son, our Great High Priest, offers himself as victim to the Father, Mary also gives the victim, her child, to the Father in union with Christ the Priest in a disposition of complete self-surrender to God.[23]

By comparison with Western developments, the Christian East seems to have given less expression to the possible redemptive significance of the sorrow of Mary, though her suffering at the cross is evoked in a relatively lengthy lamentation of the grief-stricken Mother, extant only in Latin, ascribed to the Syrian doctor, St. Ephrem. It has sometimes been called the *Stabat* of Christian antiquity.[24] The Byzantine hymnographer Romanos the Melodist has a *kontakion* on the lamenting Virgin, spoken in the name of Christ. It manifests an unease with an excessive emphasis on the sorrow of Mary, but it also ascribes to her a profound understanding of the transaction taking place on the cross.

Lay aside your grief, mother, lay it aside.

---

23. I follow the interpretative summary of a number of passages in the *Mariale* offered by Emile Druwé, "La médiation universelle de Marie. Première partie: Marie corédemptrice du genre humain," in *Maria: Études sur la sainte Vierge*, I, ed. Manoir, 427–537, and here at 512–513.

24. "Threni, id est, Lamentationes gloriosissimae Virginis Matris Mariae super Passione Domini," in *S.P.N. Ephraem Syri omnia opera quae extant, graece, syriace, latine*, III, ed. Joseph Simon Assemani (Rome, 1746), 574–575. Twentieth-century students have not found the ascription persuasive.

Lamentation does not befit you who have
been called "blessed."
Do not obscure your calling with weeping.
Do not liken yourself to those who lack
understanding, all-wise maiden.
You are in the midst of my bridal chamber.[25]

The "lamentation" (*thrênos*) of the Mother of God, regarded as a sign of her intimate association with her Son's redeeming work and not (as apparently here) a danger to that association, becomes by the eleventh century a theme in Byzantine homiletics, and both in Greece and in the East Slavonic world finds expression in visual art, much of it of stunning beauty. The German art historian Hans Belting draws attention in that context to the epigram "On the Weeping Mother of God" by the hymn writer John Mauropus (he died in or shortly before 1079), which explains the necessity of Mary's sorrow as "the way to 'resolve the cosmic grief.'"[26]

The Theme in the Roman Magisterium

This comparative lack of Oriental reflection on the role of the woman at the cross, if such it be, did not prevent the Roman magisterium from attempting some fairly audacious statements about Marian co-redemption from the middle of the nineteenth century onwards. The use of the word "co-redemption," though important, is not all-important (it chiefly characterizes the curial style of Pius X's pontificate and the personal teaching of Pius XI). Other terms,

25. See Georges Dobrot, "A Dialogue with Death: Ritual Lament and the *thrênos Theotokou* of Romanos ho Melodos," in *Greek, Roman and Byzantine Studies* 35 (1994): 385–405. The background is described in Margaret Alexiou, *The Ritual Lament in Greek Tradition* (Cambridge: Cambridge University Press, 1974). For his Mariology, see Celeste Chevalier, "Mariologie de Romanos [490–550 environ] le Roi des Mélodes," *Recherches de science religieuse* 28 (1938): 48–71.
26. Hans Belting, *Likeness and Presence* (Chicago: University of Chicago Press, 1997), 263.

especially if used cumulatively, are more or less equally capable of conveying the same idea.

To take a few examples: Leo XIII, in an encyclical written in 1894 for the fortieth anniversary of the dogmatization of the immaculate conception, describes Mary as *consors* with Christ in the "painful atonement on behalf of the human race" and "in her heart dying with him," *commoriens corde*.[27] Again, in 1904, for the fiftieth anniversary, Pius X portrays Mary suffering with her Son in such a way that "through this communion of pain and will" she merited to become the *reparatrix*, the "restorer," of a lost world, thus picking up a word that also occurs in Pius IX's bull defining the immaculate conception in 1854.[28] In a 1918 encyclical, Pius X's successor Benedict XV taught that "with every fibre of her being she immolated her Son, so that she may rightly be said to have redeemed the human race together with Christ."[29] "For this reason," the pope went on, "those graces that flow from the treasury of the Redemption are administered (*ministrantur*), as it were, through the hands of the same sorrowful Virgin"—thus linking a subjective theology of co-redemption (one concerned with the transmission of the fruits of Christ's sacrifice) to an objective theology of co-redemption (one concerned with that sacrifice in and of itself). For Pius XI, in a Marian encyclical of 1928:

> The Virgin Mother of God . . . offered the Victim of sacrifice at the foot of the Cross. Through an inscrutable and absolutely unique bond (*conjunctio*) with Christ, she shines forth conspicuously as our restorer (*reparatrix*).[30]

---

27. Leo XII, *Jucunda simper*, in *Acta Sanctae Sedis* XXVII, 128. I owe this and the following citations from texts of the papal magisterium to Miravalle, "Mary Coredemptrix, Mediatrix, Advocate: Foundational Presence in Divine Revelation" in idem. (ed.), *Mary: Coredemptrix, Mediatrix, Advocate*, 258–265.

28. Pius X, *Ad diem illum* in *Acta Sanctae Sedis*, XXXVI, 453.

29. Benedict XV, *Inter sodalicia* in *Acta Apostolicae Sedis* X, 182.

30. Pius XI, *Miserentissimus Redemptor* in ibid., XX, 178.

And in a 1935 message sent radiophonically to Lourdes this same pope, speaking in Italian, used the term *corredentrice,* "co-redemptrix," for a fifth consecutive time in the years 1933 to 1935, in a prayer which asked Mary to "preserve and increase in us" the "precious fruit of your sweet Son's redemption and [your] compassion as our Mother."[31]

Then in 1943, in a much-cited section of the well-known ecclesiological encyclical *Mystici corporis Christi* the last of the "Pian popes" Pius XII declared that Mary

> always inexorably united, *arctissime coniuncta,* with her Son, like a New Eve offered that same Son on Golgotha to the eternal Father, together with the holocaust of her maternal rights and love, on behalf of all the children of Adam. And so she, who was the physical mother of our Head, became the spiritual mother of his members also through a new title of suffering and glory.[32]

In 1950, an international Mariological congress held in Rome to mark the dogmatization of the Assumption petitioned the same pope, Pius XII, to proceed to the next steps: the dogmatization of Mary's co-redemptive role and her role as dispenser of graces—though notably it too, like the pope, avoided the actual term "co-redemptrix," asking simply that it be "dogmatically defined that the Blessed Virgin Mary was intimately associated with Christ the Saviour in effecting human salvation and is, accordingly, a true collaborator in the work of redemption." It's unclear why the last of the Pian popes backtracked on the term, by then in significant if limited papal and curial use—and in much wider theological use—for half a century. Calling Mary "co-redemptrix" could sound like making her an equal contributor to redemption with Christ rather than one who contributes to the redemption subordinately and dependently, by

---

31. Idem., "Radio Message to Lourdes," in *L'Osservatore romano,* April 29–30, 1935, 1.
32. Pius XII, *Mystici Corporis Christi,* in ibid., XXXV, 247.

participation, in a way to be described through the language of analogy.

And at the Second Vatican Council

By contrast, we know exactly why the fathers of the Second Vatican Council avoided the term "co-redemptrix" because the *Acta Synodalia* of the council tell us: it was owing to the likelihood that the word would be misunderstood by the "separated brethren": that is, for the most part, by Protestants. This might be considered slightly naïve since Protestant observers at the council made it clear at the time that the Marian eighth chapter of the Dogmatic Constitution on the Church, *Lumen gentium*, the place where the council's teaching on our Lady is found, conveyed an appreciation of Mary's role in salvation which they could not share.

Be that as it may, the text the council fathers devised speaks of Mary's "service to the mystery of redemption" in two outstanding ways which correspond to the key co-redemptive episodes of Annunciation and cross. On the first of these episodes, the Annunciation, *Lumen gentium* states:

> Rightly . . . the holy Fathers see her as used by God not merely in a passive way, but as co-operating in the work of human salvation through faith and obedience. For as St. Irenaeus says, she "being obedient, became the cause of salvation for herself and for the whole human race."[33]

Was this meant to extend also to what happened at the cross? As we have seen, there is an ambiguity here in patristic soteriology. Is the incarnation, and thus the Annunciation, its decisive moment, merely the pre-condition of redemption? Or is it itself the actual

---

33. *Lumen gentium*, 56

initiation of redemption? Or, again, does it only potentially initiate redemption through its intrinsic ordering to the Cross? Without seeking to resolve this question as far as the citation from Irenaeus and their other patristic references are concerned, the fathers of the Second Vatican Council, by the structure of the text they produced, upheld the view that Mary's Annunciation-consent was renewed at the cross and came to its climax there. At the cross, so *Lumen gentium* puts it:

> she stood, in keeping with the divine plan, suffering grievously with her only-begotten Son. There she united herself with a maternal heart to his sacrifice and lovingly consented to the immolation of the Victim she herself had brought forth.[34]

Insofar as this text, though without use of the term "co-redemptrix," orchestrates themes found in maximalist co-redemption theology, it can be described as an example of such a theology—termed "maximalist" so as to distinguish it from an alternative theology that restricts the use of co-redemption motifs to the Annunciation. Yet despite echoes of medieval and later doctrine and devotion, these two sentences offer too little in the way of theological exploration or theological construction to serve as a basis for a developed understanding of the co-redemption idea.

This restraint is easily explained. The council fathers had imposed on themselves a self-denying ordinance, formulated in *Lumen gentium* as follows:

> The Synod does not . . . have it in mind to give a complete doctrine on Mary, nor does it wish to decide those questions which have not yet been fully illuminated by the work of theologians.[35]

---

34. Ibid., 58.
35. Ibid., 54.

This was a disappointment to many of the bishops, 266 of whom—in the consultation which preceded the council—had previously asked for a dogmatic definition of the nature of Mary's contribution to Christ's saving work. The upshot was the creation of a presumption in the minds of commentators and many in the church public, especially among Catholics who had decided to make ecumenism their priority, that the magisterial trajectory of the pre-conciliar popes on Marian co-redemption had been deflected, or to put it slightly more brutally, that the conciliar majority had declared a maximalist theology of co-redemption, whether subjective or objective in character or both of these together, to be a cul-de-sac for Catholic thought. The pertinent paragraph of *Lumen gentium*, already cited, did not support that presumption.

The still wider inference could also be arrived at that the council did not want a high-profile Mariological doctrine and devotion at all, leading to what some commentators did not hesitate to describe as a "decade without Mary," stretching from 1965 to 1974.[36] 1974 was the year when Paul VI's apostolic exhortation *Marialis cultus* sought to revive the "cult of Mary" in areas of the church (notably Western Europe and North America) where that cult was flagging. Not enough note had been taken of the careful wording in which the council expressed its intention not to proceed at the present time with a so-called "fifth" Marian dogma—taking the four previous such dogmas to be the divine motherhood, the perpetual virginity, the immaculate conception, and the glorious assumption. Nor did some Catholics heed its acknowledgement of the value of earlier twentieth-century discussion of Marian co-redemption. For the council fathers had declared:

---

36. Stefano de Fiores, "Marie dans la théologie post-conciliaire," in *Vatican II: Bilan et perspectives: vingt-cinq ans après, 1962-1987*, ed. René Latourelle (Montreal: Bellarmin; Paris: Cerf, 1988), 475–478.

Those opinions may be lawfully retained which are freely propounded by schools of Catholic thought concerning her who occupies a place in the Church which is the highest after Christ and yet very close to us.[37]

The 1986 *Collectio Missarum de Beata Virgine Maria*

In the pontificate of John Paul II, the discourse of the modern popes of the pre-Conciliar period was resumed not only in the pontiff's own utterances but also by his promulgation in 1986 of a Marian collection of mass texts where much of the thematics and vocabulary of the historic sources are brought back into play. A few examples will illustrate the continuity of thought and expression compared with the co-redemptive assertions of the not-so-distant past.

For instance, the prayer over the gifts in the mass "Holy Mary, Fount of Life and Light," runs: "Holy Father, receive this oblation which, imitating the Mother of Christ, the virgin Church offers you." Or take the preface of the mass "Holy Mary at the Presentation of the Lord" which includes the words, "This is the Virgin, the minister of the saving dispensation, who offers to you the Lamb to be offered on the altar of the Cross for our salvation." Or again, the preface to the second of the two masses entitled, "The Blessed Virgin Mary, image and mother of the Church," declares, "She is the Virgin who offers, presenting the First-born in your Temple and consenting to his immolation beside the Tree of Life." I take as a final example from this mass book the opening words of the collect of the second mass "The Blessed Virgin Mary at the Cross": "O God who associated the co-suffering Mother with your suffering Son for the wonderful repairing of [our] human substance." As one student (Arthur Calkins) puts it at the end of a thorough study of these texts: "The doctrine

---

37. *Lumen gentium*, 54.

which these Masses consolidate corresponds to some of the highest points reached by the papal magisterium on our Lady."[38]

Not that they use the co-redemptrix *term*. This might be thought regrettable. The reason for favoring the reinstatement in this context of the actual term "co-redemptrix" is chiefly that a striking keyword—such as *homousios, transubstantiatio*, or, in the Marian realm, *Theotokos*—by concentrating minds is often a stimulus to doctrinal advance. At the very least, "co-redemptrix" is a convenient label for the sort of thinking represented by the various texts this section has considered.

A Dogmatic Evaluation

How, then, to understand the point dogmatically, and here I concentrate on objective theories of Marian co-redemption, since subjective theories are in the end indistinguishable from accounts of Mary as dispenser of graces through her heavenly intercession along with some reference to her relation to the church. Fundamentally, the matter divides into two: first, the *congruence* of Mary's contribution to the redemption; second, its *possibility* given that her Son is the only mediator of salvation.

In the order of congruence, fittingness, *convenientia*, the claims of objective Marian co-redemption are, it seems to me, plausible. Through his willing oblation, the Son of God brought about the perfect reconciliation by which the human race, whose new head he is, now positively deserves to become friends once more with God. That this reconciliation should be achieved by God *in our nature* rather than by mere divine decree wonderfully ennobles us as human

---

38. Arthur Burton Calkins, "Mary as Coredemptrix, Mediatrix and Advocate in the Contemporary Roman Liturgy," in *Mary: Coredemptrix, Mediatrix, Advocate*, ed. Mark Maraville, 111, whose presentation of these liturgical texts I follow.

beings. It is the soteriological basis of our regained dignity as made in the image of God. However, the one who achieved our salvation was himself a divine person acting in human nature, not—compare Cyril of Alexandria against Nestorius, and the christological definitions of Chalcedon and Constantinople II—a human person. That the New Adam should have a helpmate in the achieving of salvation who was a human person befits the structure of salvation and, if this is a female human person we are talking about, enhances the symmetry of redemption as the inversion of the fall. Part of the beauty of redemption lies in the way God led man back to his friendship by a path corresponding to that by which man had forsaken it—hence the New Adam with his helpmate, the New Eve. So much for fittingness.

But, congruence aside, can a constituent role for Mary in the putting in place of objective redemption really be possible, granted the uniqueness of Christ's mediation of salvation? It *can* be possible on the principle *causa causae est causa causatae*, "the cause of a cause is the cause of what is caused." Thanks to the unique plenitude of grace given her at her conception, the role Mary played—not one of divine motherhood for *just any* incarnation, but divine motherhood specifically for a *redemptive* incarnation—was bestowed on her through the anticipated merits of her Son: the Father willing it, the Holy Spirit bringing it about. It was the Son who meritoriously caused the distinguishing role she was to play. Her initial sanctification, then, was inherently oriented not just to the incarnation event, but, more than that, to the *purpose* of the incarnation—to its *redemptive* purpose. And so the order of redemption includes not only the divine person of the Word made flesh but also a human person who has been raised to the dignity of a helpmate fit for him in his redeeming work: a mother who will become for the sake of human salvation, a spiritually active companion at the crucial moment of redemption, the moment of the cross.

A Marian dogma formulated along these lines would not detract from the uniqueness of the work of Christ. Indeed, it could be presented as advancing our understanding of the fruitfulness of that work. By causing Mary to act for the sake of his mission in earth, the Savior demonstrated his redemptive power more fully than had he lacked such an *adiutrix*. He extended the sense in which the saving plan was to enhance the dignity of humankind without any diminution of the exclusivity of his own action, since "the cause of a cause is the cause of what is caused." Mary's cooperation added nothing to the intrinsic value of Christ's sacrifice, but by her offering of the divine-human victim, humanity in her made its own the supreme act of reparation which only Christ could put in place.

Her supportive contribution consists, then, of the costing ratification of the offering of Christ by a human person. It took the form of a dolorous offering of the offering—and so can be called a co-oblation, always understanding that we use the term "co-oblation" analogically, to mark the subordinate, dependent, and participatory character of her involvement. Whereas the first Eve by her disobedience solicited the old Adam to total soteriological ruin, the New Eve, in her perfect obedience, ratifies the Second Adam in his achieving of all saving good. In this, the compassion of the Mother of God contributed directly to producing the effects we call the overall objective redemption as it transpires before God. Accordingly, the Pseudo-Albert's *Mariale* put matters appropriately when its unknown author declared that the bonding of the world to God by the Lord's passion is suitably echoed in its bonding to our Lady by her compassion.

This universality of significance, it can be said, is why, in the words of the American Mariologist Mark Miravalle: "The corpus of

Marian dogma will not be complete until the Church presents a dogma directly defining the nature of Mary's co- redemptive mission with the Redeemer."[39] A celebrated reviewer's gaffe runs: "This book fills a much-needed gap." Such a dogma, arguably, is needed to fill a gap between what the Catholic Church defined in 1854 about Mary's beginnings and what she defined in 1950 about Mary's end. It is because the *Immaculata* took part co-redemptively in the saving struggle of her Son with sin and death that the church knows her to have shared in his triumph over sin and its consequences—the assumption.

---

39. "Introduction" in *Mary: Coredemptrix, Mediatrix, Advocate,* ed. Mark Maraville, xiii. This sentence ends, "and her corresponding ecclesial relation to us in the order of grace," a reference to the further mysteries of Mary's mediation of graces and motherhood of the church.

5

The Assumption

A helpful way into the topic, I find, is to formulate the following question: In what sense does the dogma of the assumption rest on evidence? In the years of build-up to the proclamation of the dogma in 1950, Catholic theologians differed about this question in interesting ways. We might do worse than to begin from here.

Questions of Method

On one influential account, the assumption doctrine could be dogmatized—in other words, defined as a truth of faith which all the faithful are obliged to hold—simply because in a certain way it is an inference from other truths in the doctrinal corpus, some of them already dogmatically in place. On the most respectable version of this view: the assumption of the Mother of God is virtually revealed—meaning not, of course, "almost revealed," but that it is revealed by virtue of its tacit containment within other truths that are themselves actually revealed: passed down explicitly as revelation is transmitted. Such "containment" is something theologians saw it as part of their task to describe. On this view, there is no need to investigate in Scripture and tradition possible grounds for the truth of the belief in the assumption. Appeal to such grounds is, strictly speaking, unnecessary. All that is needed is that other relevant true beliefs are appropriately grounded in Scripture and tradition, and that these truths, either taken singly, in some one instance, or together, by some combination among themselves, tacitly include belief in Mary's assumption.

As we shall see, whether or not this approach is correct, it certainly identifies how best to explore the *meaning* of the assumption belief—how to bring out its content and its place within Christian truth as a whole. That is because to regard the assumption as tacitly included in the ambit of revealed truths is, among other things, to locate it by means of the "analogy of faith." As we saw in the opening chapter, to investigate the bearings of some datum of Scripture and tradition (or perhaps, in the case under consideration, some corollary of data in Scripture and tradition), we need to relocate that datum (or that corollary) within the totality of revelation as a whole. That is a key feature of the recipe for theological method found in the Constitution on Faith of the First Vatican Council.

Does that mean, then, that the memory of the church, or at least—so as not to prejudge the matter in hand—the *alleged* memory, to the effect that the Mother of the Lord was given a unique destiny in the plan of God counts for nothing in this enquiry? That would be strange because, at the time of the preparation of the assumption dogma, other writers were simultaneously engaged in arguing that, beginning with the Apocalypse of St. John (the celebrated scene of the Woman clothed with the Sun in chapter twelve of that book), the church had externalized an interior memory in tangible monuments: in texts, practices, artworks. That inner memory was outwardly embodied most obviously, so it was said, in the development of the liturgical feast of the assumption, and in the feast's own expression in homilies and iconography. It was also, and more controversially, embodied in an unwieldy body of literature produced in a variety of languages from Armenian through Coptic to Old Irish, a corpus of texts known as the *Transitus Mariae*—the "Transits of Mary"—accounts of Mary's passage from this world to the next.[1] Strange as it may be to think that this range of texts and objects could be disregarded by seekers after the truth of the assumption, the austerely-minded dogmaticians with whom I began could be taken as recommending precisely that. One might well bypass completely this literary corpus (and its accompanying iconographic repertoire).

A possible attraction of that approach to some was being let off the hook of trying to sort out the interrelations of texts in the notoriously unmanageable *Transitus* literature. A sigh of relief might follow the lifting of the burden of working out the theological intentions and presuppositions of the authors of that literature, the chronological order of composition of the texts (as computed if not by absolute dating then by reference to their mutual relations), as well as the location of their origins (was it in the Great Church, or, alternatively, in heretical or even gnosticizing milieu?). No longer did one have to worry about what for the empirically minded was the key issue—the

---

1. For surveys, see Martin Jugie, "Assomption de la Sainte Vierge," in *Maria: Études sur la sainte Vierge*, I, ed. Manoir, 619–658, for whom the combination of Apocrypha and "pious seers" with a small number of patristic references constitutes a "legendarium," but nothing historically dependable; Stephen J. Shoemaker, *Ancient Traditions of the Virgin Mary's Dormition and Assumption* (Oxford: Oxford University Press, 2002) has a characteristically postmodern animus against attempting any "globalising" harmonization of the traditions; Édouard Cothenet, "Marie dans les Apocryphes," in *Maria: Études sur la sainte Vierge*, VI, ed. Manoir, 71–156, is more sympathetic to the *Transitus* literature, seeking to establish its most ancient kernel, which he locates so far as literary texts are concerned around 300, but ascribes in a pre-literary way to the late second century when interest in the last moments of figures around Jesus (notably the apostles) became common.

historical value (or lack of it) of the *Transitus Mariae* texts vis-à-vis the earthly facts of Mary's last hours and the fate of her physical remains.

We should note, though, that the phrase "the historical value or lack of it of the *Transitus* literature" is itself ambiguous. It *could* mean, the evidential value of this literature for what happened to Mary's body. It could *also* mean, the evidential value of this literature for the state of the church's faith at the time of the composition of these texts—so far as questions of Mary's destiny were concerned. What to a theologian the phrase "the historical value or lack of it of the *Transitus* literature" should *never* mean, however—and this goes for the other pertinent monuments of tradition as well—is their evidential value for the mystery of the assumption *in and of itself*. That mystery concerns divine acts transforming definitively the status of the ontological elements (body and soul, or flesh and spirit) that entered into the making of Mary's personhood. Those divine acts escape the bounds of natural human enquiry of any kind. That is so, of course, because the kind of agency involved is eschatological and Trinitarian, and so can hardly be factored into any naturally derived formula, never mind a purely empiricist one. The action concerned is what God the Trinity is doing to consummate the existence of the Mother of Jesus.

Here the situation of the assumption is parallel to that of the exaltation of Christ in his resurrection and ascension. These are events with two poles, one of which is constituted by the space and time with which we are familiar, while the other belongs to another kind of spatiality and duration—a kind that expresses the conclusive purpose of the triune God in bringing his plan to its final condition. There could in theory be evidence that Mary's mortal body disappeared from view, just as there could be evidence that the Easter tomb was empty. But there could never be evidence that the Mother of the Lord at the end of her earthly life was taken forward immediately to the last condition of the consummated creature, just as, similarly, there could never be evidence that the human nature assumed body and soul by the uncreated Word now exists in God in a condition of unspeakable exaltation. These truths, if they really are truths, can only be made known by the impact of the self-revealing word of God on human faculties, faculties working in rational and imaginative responsiveness to that same Word in the cognitive process by which we come to know revelation in and for itself.

In identifying three possible senses of the phrase "the historical value . . . of the *Transitus* literature" I distinguish first, then, empirical investigation from another kind of historical enquiry whose object is not the fate of Mary's body within the organic continuum but the faith of the church about what happened to Mary's body within that continuum including her body's possible reanimation by her soul. And I distinguish, secondly, from both these two forms of enquiry the divinely enabled faith-awareness which registers the actual assumption event (if such there were) in the revelation consciousness of the church. In the latter case, the bi-polarity of the assumption event (it takes place on the threshold between our world and the next), by situating that event not just in our space and time but in what space and time now are for God in Christ, guarantees that here only a fully theological epistemology will serve our turn.

At the time of the preparation of the assumption dogma, all Catholic theologians would have agreed that enquiry on the natural level, empiricst or otherwise, could never verify the assumption. Where they disagreed, as I have said, was on the value to be accorded an enquiry into literary evidence (evidence in written texts, and, to a lesser degree, the illustration of those texts in objects of art), if such evidence be considered as direct testimony to the contents of the church's memory—the memory of a revelation made to her in the apostles' lifetime.

For there was, so we have seen, an alternative road down which theology could travel. The assumption could be conceived as, quite simply, tacitly contained in other aspects of the church's faith.

The Meaning of the Phrase "the Assumption"

So far in this discussion it has been taken for granted that we are all agreed on what the phrase "the assumption" means. But is this a justified supposition on my part? In actual fact, at the time of the dogmatization the core meaning of the phrase "the assumption" was deliberately left open in one crucial respect. I echoed that indeterminacy when I referred to the "earthly facts of Mary's last hours and the fate of her physical remains." It was not the fate of the physical remains that was disputed so much as what transpired in her "last hours." Specifically, did she die? The majority opinion was and is that Mary underwent the death of the body and its separation from the soul. However, a minority view to the contrary was deemed respectable, represented as it was in the Franciscan theological tradition and upheld by the individual who was possibly the single most influential theological adviser to Pius XII on Marian questions, the French Assumptionist Martin Jugie. The crucial words of the 1950 dogmatic definition would run:

> We pronounce, declare, and define it to be a divinely revealed dogma that the Immaculate Mother of God, the ever-virgin Mary, having completed the course of her earthly life, was assumed body and soul into heaven by glory.

"Having completed the course of her earthly life," *expleto terrestris vitae cursu*, is a phrase intended to satisfy both Mortalists and

Immortalists: both those who held that Mary certainly died as we die and—most importantly—as her Son died (those were the Mortalists) and also those others (the Immortalists) who considered that intrinsic to the uniqueness of her destiny was her passing in uninterrupted fashion from a mortal to an immortal condition—participating in that way in the deathlessness which, after the events of the resurrection and ascension, characterized the particular human substance she had given at the Annunciation to the uncreated Word—the humanity of Jesus as now existing with the Father. Whereas immortalism is almost totally absent from the *Transitus* literature,[2] Mortalism, sometimes in an extreme form postulating for Mary a sojourn of up to two hundred days in the tomb, is overwhelmingly dominant there. So immortalist theologians of the assumption have often been among those most hostile to regarding the ancient accounts of Mary's passing as historically evidential—even in the restricted sense that such accounts were valuable testimonies to the faith of the earlier church. Immortalists could and did speak of the *Transitus* texts as though they were an incubus, an encumbrance, an embarrassment, and in this they joined hands with a variety of critics of the proposed dogmatization who had other grounds for querying it: including the historical skeptics, and opponents of supernatural or revealed religion of any kind. This was a curious alliance, one might say, between devotees of the highest Mariology and supporters of the lowest, formed on the basis of hostility to a body of often bizarre but sometimes also inspirational texts from the late patristic world.

2. Most theological testimonies to immortalism, it was claimed, date from between the seventeenth and nineteenth centuries: thus J. Galot, "Le Mystère de l'Assomption," in *Maria: Études sur la sainte Vierge*, VII, ed. Manoir, 190.

The Assumption and the Analogy of Faith

I began this chapter by drawing attention to what I called the approach of the most "austerely minded dogmaticians" (such as Reginald Garrigou-Lagrange) for whom the truth of the assumption could be established without any reference to its possible direct—as distinct from indirect—foundations in Scripture and tradition, and I suggested that their approach was valuable at least in this sense: by directing our gaze to the interrelations which join the assumption belief to other areas of doctrine that approach grants us an entrée to the *meaning* of this dogma, its significance within the wider world of Christian doctrine as a whole. Whether the partisans of that approach in its purest form went too far by taking it also to establish the dogma's truth, to the exclusion of any interest in direct witness to it from Scripture and tradition, is another matter.

So how did Catholic theologians understand the relation of this doctrine to other doctrinal areas, and notably, in the first instance, to other Marian doctrines, some already dogmatized, like the divine motherhood of Mary, and some not, like her co-redemptive role?

An informative account of the inter-relation of assumption faith to other aspects of Marian doctrine is found in an essay in the respected American journal *The Thomist* from 1951, in a fascicule intended to mark the proclamation of the new dogma.[3] The author of "The Assumption among Mary's Privileges," a Carmelite of the Ancient Observance in their Washington study house, Whitefriars, managed in short compass to survey many other writers on this subject in the Catholic theological tradition, and I shall make full use of his material now.

---

3. Kilian Healey, "The Assumption among Mary's Privileges," *The Thomist* 14 (1951): 72-92.

i. The Assumption and the Divine Motherhood

In the second chapter we saw that the most important of the Marian doctrines, and the first to be defined, was the divine motherhood: Mary is the *Theotokos* as proclaimed at Ephesus in St. Cyril's great moment of triumph. So Kilian Healey's essay quite properly begins here. In "The Assumption among Mary's Privileges," Healey considers how to evaluate the relation of assumption belief to the divine motherhood understood as, in his words, "not only the physical act of conception and generation of the Son of God, but the supernatural and meritorious consent which preceded [that] conception and the consequent quasi-infinite dignity that necessarily accompanied it"—a quasi-infinite dignity (the phrase echoes words of Thomas in the *Prima Pars*) which in Thomist Mariology, building as this does on a Cyrilline Christology, has its explanation in the way Mary at the Annunciation entered the hypostatic order and not just the order of grace, since at that moment it began to be true of her person that she was directly related to one of the Trinitarian hypostases themselves.

As Healey shows, some Catholic theologians, writing between the two world wars when literature on the assumption reached its peak, argued that the assumption is virtually revealed in the divine motherhood of Mary alone, and they understood that virtuality in the sense of what Neo-Scholastics of the period called "formal implicit revelation." A truth was handed down tacitly, not explicitly, but it could be rendered explicit simply by analysis of what was contained in a truth handed down not tacitly but explicitly. Such was the meaning of the phrase "formally implicitly revealed." Analysis of the notion of divine motherhood, such writers said, will lead inescapably to the conclusion that Mary's final end must be as assumption belief understands it.

Their argument ran like this. The perfect filial love of Jesus for his mother, unavoidable in a divine hypostasis who took human nature as a mother's son, renders it inconceivable that the God-man would "allow [Mary] to suffer the dishonour of permanence in death when he could easily and in harmony with her dignity glorify her body in heaven immediately after death."[4] Though noting this opinion respectfully, Healey was inclined to support, rather, those theologians who described the assumption as, in its relation to the divine motherhood, "supremely fitting," *maxime conveniens*. It was, he wrote, "indeed most fitting that the body of Our Lady—made sacred by her contact with divinity when she gave of her own substance to form the flesh of the Word Incarnate—be preserved from the dishonour of corruption and permanence in death." Further than this he would not go, citing (allusively) the principle laid down by the prophet Isaiah that God's ways are not necessarily man's ways. As Healey puts it: "[W]ho can measure the love of Jesus for his Mother and determine the exact way in which Jesus must manifest his love?"[5] In point of fact, in Pius XII's bull defining the assumption dogma, *Munificentissimus Deus*, still being drafted when Healey wrote, the divine motherhood would seemingly be taken as so grounding the assumption that its truth could be magisterially defined on that basis alone. Much is made in the bull of the prayer *Veneranda* inserted into the Roman formularies around 620 by the Syrian pope Sergius I. It is a prayer that presents the assumption as a necessary consequence of the divine motherhood: the assumption event was due to the Mother of the Lord since she had provided from herself the matter for the incarnation of the Son of God.

4. Ibid, 77.
5. Ibid.

ii. The Assumption and the Immaculate Conception

The divine motherhood was not, however, the only dogma to which the assumption could be related in the analogy of faith. What, for instance, of the relation between Mary's assumption and her immaculate conception? Once again, the strongest or most daring view was that assumption belief was "formally implicitly" contained in the doctrine dogmatized in 1854. Examination of the very idea of Mary's preservative redemption, producing in her as it does a condition of original righteousness, can be shown to generate of itself (so the claim goes) the grounds for holding the assumption thesis as true.

Our Carmelite guide, however, found distinctly unsatisfactory the arguments put forward to this end, notably by Martin Jugie, the Byzantinist with a special interest in things Mariological already mentioned. For Jugie, it belongs to the logic of the divine plan disclosed in Scripture that whoever has always been exempt from every sin—supposing there to be at least one such individual human person in the course of history—has a right to enjoy a glorious immortality for body and soul immediately after death or, better still, immediately after the end of their earthly probation, a phrase which kept the door open for Immortalism. Now Mary of Nazareth has always been exempt from sin in every sense. Ergo, she had a right to a glorious resurrection or, as Jugie would prefer to say, to immortality: that is, to non-subjection to death. But to this, so Healey pointed out, an objection may be made. While Mary's redemption was preservative it was nevertheless redemption. Consequently, she never had a *right* to the state of justice, with its exclusion of death as we know it, that belonged to Adam before the fall.

Indeed, one could go further than Healey in this direction, and add that the condemnation of Adam has now been englobed in the higher order of the work of Christ's salvation, such that Mary's privilege of immaculacy in conception exempts her from original sin not to return her to the Adamic state but, rather, to introduce her more profoundly into the redeeming work of her Son achieved as this was precisely in and through dying. (We saw in the last chapter how Schillebeeckx too protested against treating the Mother of God as an "extra-Christian child of Paradise.")

Moreover (and now returning to Healey), while it is true that as a result of her exemption from sin, Mary has the right not to suffer death *qua punishment for sin*, that does not mean she has a right to avoid death and the grave *as such*. In point of fact, affirms Healey who, unlike Jugie, was a Mortalist, she *did* die. God willed the death of Mary precisely because of the intimacy of her association with her Son, Jesus Christ. As is wonderfully expressed in the Byzantine liturgy for the assumption,[6] it was deeply appropriate that the Mother should follow the paschal road taken by the Son[7]—a deep appropriateness which later Catholic theologians would contemplate in the mirror of her role as co-redemptrix. According to Healey, the role of co-redemptrix implies Mary's death, since her dying was part and parcel of her conformation to the passion of Christ.[8] That co-redemptive role does not, though, require her permanence in death. Permanence in death or corruption would be, he writes, of no conceivable spiritual advantage to her or to humankind.[9]

6. In Byzantine Christianity the more usual term is the "Falling Asleep" of the Mother of God, in Greek *koimêsis*, in Latin *dormitio*, though the word *analêpsis*, an exact equivalent of *assumptio*, is not unknown.

7. Thus it could be argued, from the starting point of the definition of the immaculate conception in *Ineffabilis Deus*, that if the New Eve is victorious over Satan she must be so not only in escaping the effects of sin but also in escaping not indeed death itself but at any rate "the kingdom of death by a resurrection and a corporal Assumption, just as Christ did": Joseph Duhr, *The Glorious Assumption of the Mother of God* (London: Burns Oates, 1951), 84.

8. In fairness to the Immortalists it should be said they were by no means impervious to this argument, but Jugie proposed that Mary's configuration to Christ crucified took place in her "dolorous compassion" on Calvary when she became the Queen of Martyrs: thus M. Jugie, "Assomption de la Sainte Vierge," art. cit., p. 621.

But even if, *pace* Jugie, the assumption is not contained—formally implicitly—within the immaculate conception dogma, we can still posit a harmonious connexion between assumption and immaculate conception. Indeed, for Healey, there is rather more than a harmonious connexion. There is here an exigence, or what in Neo-Scholastic parlance is termed a "necessitating convenience," since the contrary of the thesis concerned—the denial that Mary's immaculate conception called for her assumption—is *inconveniens*: that is, unfitting to the plan of God. As Healey writes:

> In the first place, does not the immaculate soul of Mary, free from the corrupting power of concupiscence [the tendency of fallen man to moral evil] demand as a natural complement an immaculate body that is free from even the corruption of the grave [the archetypal physical evil, at any rate for the Greek patristic tradition]? And secondly, since God has preserved Our Lady from sin, would He not also preserve her from the positive punishment of sin: the return of the body to the dust of the earth?[10]

And to these questions we are of course expected to answer, Yes.

And yet these are still only arguments from fittingness, albeit maximal fittingness. An argument for the strict entailment of the assumption doctrine in the conception dogma was provided by the Fribourg Thomist, Charles Journet, writing four years after the 1950 papal action. In First Corinthians 15, St. Paul transmits a revealed

---

9. We shall return to the relation of the assumption to the co-redemption but meanwhile we can note how Healey's observation that Mary's permanence in death or corruption would be of no spiritual advantage to human beings flags up the issue of her dispensation of grace and her role vis-à-vis the church, which are the themes of the next two chapters. Our Lady's non-permanence in death, and non-permanence in corruption, are, precisely, spiritually advantageous to mankind. Her realized eschatological condition as, in contrast to the saints, gloriously alive in her entire personal being (the body included), such that she was superbly fulfilled in union with her Son: this qualifies her to be both the supreme intercessor with him and also the icon of the church as the church will be at the end of time. In Schillebeeckx's words, "Her resurrection is the 'constitution in power' of her motherhood with regard to all men," thus Schillebeeckx, *Mary Mother of the Redemption*, 118.
10. Healey, art. cit., p. 79.

teaching: all who are members of Christ will be co-glorified with him in a transformation that, however, for everyone touched by sin, is postponed until the moment at the end of the world when the reign of sin is finally destroyed. From this we can infer, writes Journet, that for any member of Christ untouched by personal or original sin (there is one, the Mother of the Lord) the law of co-glorification with Christ would come into effect immediately upon their death. And with her this was so.[11]

iii. The Assumption and Mary's Virginity and Holiness

Leaving now the topic of relation to the immaculate conception, Healey also reports that Mariologists had sought to interrelate the assumption to two further privileges disclosed at the Annunciation event—Mary's virginity, understood here as a divinely conferred vocation of perpetual virginity, and Mary's holiness, understood as the gift of a unique plenitude of sanctifying grace. We can take each of these in turn. For some writers, corporeal incorruption is the highest perfection of virginal incorruption. Between these terms—virginal incorruption, corporeal incorruption—the common factor is the integrity of the body, but of course the discussion is really about that virginal body *that was the temple of the Word*. The Virgin Mary's body should rightly have enjoyed incorruption. Yet bodily incorruption without anticipated resurrection would be unintelligible. Hence the assumption follows.

Healey hesitates in regard to the assertion that physical incorruptibility without resurrection has to be considered meaningless. On the contrary, he says, we know from hagiology that such incorruptibility is a grace given to the bodies of some of

---

11. Journet, *Esquisse du développement du dogme marial*, 138–140.

the saints. It must, therefore, even without anticipated resurrection, have a soteriological rationale of some kind—whatever we take that rationale to be. So, he concludes, "it is difficult to hold as certain that [Mary's] virginity *necessarily demands* the assumption for its highest perfection." The Byzantine doctors, in their homilies on the dormition, may associate with the assumption Mary's perpetual virginity, and notably her *virginitas in partu*, but they do not treat this connexion as one of entailment.

What about the implications, if any, the assumption of Mary's unique endowment with sanctifying grace, as expressed in the *kecharitōmenē* of Gabriel's greeting, and confirmed by Elisabeth's cry of amazement at the visitation, "Blessed art thou among women"—two key segments of the frequently repeated prayer called the "Hail Mary." Healey is sympathetic to the claim that Mary's assumption is formally implicitly revealed in these affirmations of her fullness of grace and exceptional blessing. The argument runs: such fullness of grace and exceptional blessing exempt Mary from divine malediction. Yet according to Genesis 3, the divine malediction visited on mankind in the exclusion from Eden includes for all human mothers the pain of childbirth and for all human beings corruption in the grave. If Mary is exempt from divine malediction as a whole she was also exempt from these, which are among its constitutive parts.

The doyen of Dominican theologians at midcentury, Reginald Garrigou-Lagrange, was among the commentators who judged that we have here an example not merely of a logical deduction from revealed truths (a "theological conclusion") but a theological explanation of a truth that really is formally implicitly revealed with, in, and through the disclosure of Mary's holiness in the Lucan dialogues that accompany the Annunciation and visitation. As such, the assumption belongs to revelation proper, rather than being simply a logical deduction from revelation through the application of dialectic. If you'd asked the apostles, Did holy Mary have to escape the bonds of death?, they would have answered affirmatively without hesitation. If you'd enquired of the sub-apostolic church and later, the predominant view would be—even without theologians to construct an argument—"That sounds right."

iv. The Assumption and the Co-redemption

Where the force for assumption belief of the other Marian privileges is concerned, that might be considered the end of the story. But in fact Healey has a further card up his sleeve. It is the co-redemption which he plays as the trump card in the game. The co-redemption or, as he puts it, Mary's association with Christ in his redemptive sacrifice, is for him the source of an argument that enjoys the greatest demonstrative power for the truth of assumption belief. It is because Mary is associated with her Son, as the New Eve, helpmate of the New Adam in his struggle with evil—a term that embraces not only Satan, sin, and concupiscence but also death, that she ought to be associated with her Son in his complete victory over death—and this will take the form, then, of anticipated resurrection, or what tradition calls her assumption. Healey is able to cite Garrigou-Lagrange again since the Grand Old Man of Neo-Thomism had already declared this to be the decisive argument in favor of Mary's glorification. If the co-redemption did not issue in the assumption, then, in Healey's words, the parallelism between Christ and Mary ceased at Calvary. Whereas Christ by his resurrection had conquered evil radically in all its forms, the Mother of God, still held by the bonds of death, would remain—to that extent—in Satan's power. Linking the assumption to the co-redemption has the advantage of making plain that what we are dealing with here is the paschal pattern: through the cross to glory.

More widely, to take the assumption in close connexion with the co-redemption should be to locate it not merely within the restricted inner circle of Marian beliefs found in the church but within the wider outer circle of revelation as a whole, the centre of which is the redeeming Christ, the sacrificed Lamb who, by his enactment on the cross of the love that goes on forever in the divine Trinity, is glorious in the Father's sight.

To confine the assumption, or any other Marian doctrine for that matter, to the circle of Mary's privileges, as does the Carmelite writer I have been following, is to do it a disservice inasmuch as such an account manifestly lacks the Christocentricity intrinsic to New Testament revelation at large. The language of Marian "privileges" obscures the fact that what are called privileges are really stages in an unfolding mission, itself to be described by its service to the economy of the Son and, in dependence on that economy, in its relation to the work of the Spirit. One of the services which *ressourcement* theology performed in relation to Neo-Scholasticism in the 1940s and 50s was to restore the predominantly Christocentric focus of the Fathers, which also means, ultimately, their Trinitarian focus, because, as the Swiss dogmatician Hans Urs von Balthasar—himself a product of *ressourcement* theology—declares, Christ is always the "Trinitarian Son," constitutively related to the Father and the Spirit as well as to the Word whose hypostasis he bears as his own.[12]

Like any doctrine concerning Mary, the assumption needs to be shown in a Christocentric light. Supporters of what I've been calling the austere dogmatic approach, those who sought to extract the content of the assumption dogma from other doctrines (especially already defined doctrines) held by the contemporary Catholic Church, could have learned that more full-blooded Christocentric

---

12. Compare Hans Urs von Balthasar, *Theodramatik II/2: Die Personen in Christus* (Einsiedeln: Johannes Verlag, 1978), 198.

way of practicing Mariology from the patristic and mediaeval sources (notable Byzantine) to which they were comparatively indifferent. One has to except here (at any rate in part) Martin Jugie, who combined with his Neo-Scholasticism a breathtaking expertise as an historical theologian and especially as an Orientalist. Yet the Neo-Scholastic tail on Jugie seems to have wagged the neo-patristic dog.

The rhetoric of the early homilies on Mary's dormition, like the descriptions of her death and glorification in the *Transitus* accounts, rests on a correct doctrinal principle drawn from that wider Christocentrically defined circle of revelation tenets to which I just referred. Both the early homilies and the *Transitus Mariae* understand Mary's final destiny chiefly by analogy with that of her Son. Admittedly, this analogy is limited. She is a human person, he is a divine person. She is passive in her raising to glory; he is sovereignly active in his triumph since though his power (like all he has) is received from the Father he holds it in his own person and exercises it by himself albeit in common with the Father and the Spirit. Yet for all that, the analogy is basically valid: the glorious end of Mary is a mystery comprising at its own level an equivalent to Christ's resurrection and ascension—the reanimation of her body and hence its reunion with her soul and the spiritualization or transformation of the whole person by the fullness of divine life, involving her raising up to be with God in a fashion which imitates Christ's "session," his seating at the Father's right hand. As the Belgian Jesuit Jean Galot put it, in Christ, the resurrection was a triumph of life over death, while the ascension was his taking possession of his heavenly rule and entry on his condition of intercessor for us with the Father. In Mary, correspondingly, the assumption is not only the suffusion of her entire person with the divine life (compare Easter). It is also the gift to her of a share in her Son's sovereignty (hence her "Queenship," celebrated on the Octave Day of the Assumption in the Roman rite) and a share too in his intercessor role (compare the ascension).

The Strange Silence of Neo-Scholasticism about the "Deep Memory" of the Church

The peculiarity (in the pejorative sense) of the Neo-Scholastic theology of the assumption was, surely, its comparative lack of interest in historical enquiry, as though the deep consciousness of the Church could only contain a sense of the inner coherence of revelation and not any actual memory of revelational events. Of course it was understood that, at any rate by spiritual exegesis, and if possible by literal, Scripture had to be invoked in some way. Here the twelfth chapter of the Apocalypse was pertinent—though, surprisingly, the pope would make no reference to it in the bull.[13] The materials from tradition were, however, kept distinctly at arm's length.

It is only fair to add that notable church historians not infrequently supported the Neo-Scholastics in their approach here, for such historians feared claims would otherwise be made for a continuity of assumption believing that would bring Catholic historical scholarship into disrepute in the learned world. The marked aversion of modern Scholastics, like some of their early mediaeval predecessors, to the *Transitus* accounts which, despite their naïveté, vehicled, for the most part, the basic paschal pattern of salvation and so preserved a strong Christological reference, was perhaps understandable given the

---

13. See Jugie, "Assomption de la sainte Vierge," art. cit., who points out that since of the apostolic witnesses only John the Divine was, in all probability, still alive, the isolated character of this text is not surprising. In Jugie's reading the relevant verses describe the *Assumpta* as vested in the sun as with a royal mantle, in conformity to Jesus's logion in Matt. 13:43, "The just will shine like the sun in the Kingdom of their Father." Typically, he saw the woman's flight on "eagle's wings" as indicating that Mary never actually died, ibid., 630.

legendary cast of these texts and their contradictions with one another. The question of their inter-relationships is a topic of extraordinary complexity which has by no means elicited a scholarly consensus even today when the progress of the academic research industry and the concomitant ease of consulting sources and monographs should have advanced the discussion in the direction of substantial agreement—or so one might think. But what the *Transitus Mariae* texts did in the history of the church was to stimulate the development of a faith intuition and the consecration of that intuition in the liturgies of both East and West. The approach of Jugie's younger confrere, the Byzantinist Antoine Wenger, was to hold that though the documents are murky streams, their waters carry with them occasional nuggets of gold.[14] The intuition the *Transitus* accounts triggered was not, I suggest, simply a perception of coherence—the coherence between the assumption doctrine and other Marian or, more widely, christological, tenets—or, rather, if it *were* such a perception of coherence in the case under consideration it must *also* have been the recreation in the ecclesial memory of an event. I say that because the truth in question, for which coherence is certainly *one* criterion, is fundamentally a truth-claim about what happened to a particular someone at a particular time in a particular place—even if, to do justice to that event, its placing in the space-time continuum we share as humans on the surface of this planet must also be related to the other pole, its location in the ultimate space-time of God's consummated creation.

Catholic theology has to dare to take seriously the signs of that sporadically reviviscent ecclesial memory: in the Book of the Apocalypse, in the beginnings of the festal commemoration,[15] in the *Transitus* accounts,[16] in the homilies of Oriental bishops both Melchite

14. Antoine Wenger, *L'assomption de la très sainte Vierge dans la tradition Byzantine du VIe au Xe siècle* (Paris: Institut français d'études byzantines, 1955).

and Miaphysite (Monophysite), and—not least—the intriguing fact that the only Marian relics known to the patristic Church were her robe and her girdle.[17] She had not abandoned the body. She had only (such was the memory) stepped out of her garments and slipped away. Rainer Maria Rilke, who had been brought up as a Catholic in the old Habsburg Empire, put it as follows in his poem "The Death of Mary":

> Lo, like sweet lavender, and buried in its sweetness,
> herein was laid awhile full lowly she,
> so that the earth in many-folding creases
> like a fine cloth henceforth of her may smell.
> All what is dead (thou feelest), what deceases
> is come within her fragrance' heavy spell.
> Look at the linen, more dazzling the tissues
> than when a fuller bleaches all away!
> This light from the unsullied corpse that issues
> had more of purging in't than the sun's ray.
> But see, who softly she her leave hath taken!
> almost as twere she still, there's not a thing
> displaced. But overhead the heavens are shaken.
> Man, on thy knees and look tow'rd me and sing.[18]

15. Was the Christmastide "Memory" (*Mnéme*) of Mary (we have already considered this at Alexandria in connection with Athanasius and the divine motherhood), deemed by the great Austrian historian of the early liturgy Anton Baumstark to be kept at Antioch by 370 and known to Proclus of Constantinople in the East Roman capital a century later, already a celebration of Mary's entry into heaven—and not just her role in the incarnation? When around 600 the emperor Maurice ordered the feast of her *Koimêsis* to be celebrated on August 15 this may well have been the assigning of a day, not the inauguration of a novelty. Interestingly, the date chosen fits well enough with the legend of 200 days between her death and her assumption in the Coptic accounts. In Rome the feast of the dormition was known in Rome under Pope Sergius I (687–701); in the eighth century its name was altered to that of the *Adsumptio*.

16. We cannot rule out the "ever-present possibility that it ['the apocryphal literature of the early church'] is reproducing old and half-forgotten traditions": William O'Shea, "The History of the Feast of the Assumption," *The Thomist* XIV (1951): 118–132, and here at p. 121.

17. For the Blachernae church as sanctuary of these relics, see Raymond Janin, *La géographie ecclésiastique de l'Empire byzantine I. Le siège de Constantinople et le patriarcat oeuménique 3. Les églises et les monastères* (Paris: Institut français d'études byzantines, 1969),163–169.

18. Rainer Maria Rilke, The Life of the Virgin Mary, translated by G. L. Barrett (Wuerzburg, 1921), p. 27.

6

————

Mediatrix of Graces

I call this chapter "Mediatrix of Graces," not "Mediatrix of *all* Graces," which is the more usual form of this Marian title: Why I do so should eventually become apparent.

Recapitulation of Two Useful Distinctions

In the fourth chapter, on the co-redemption, I explained how it is customary to distinguish between Mary's cooperation in the objective redemption and her associated role in subjective redemption. That is a distinction between what she contributed to the putting in place of the divine redemptive act whose chief moments are the incarnation and the atonement—the objective redemption, and the part she plays in communicating the fruits of that act—the subjective redemption. Objective redemption is the constitution of the redemptive act; subjective redemption is its application to human subjects. Under the Marian title of co-redemptrix we considered the first of these topics, leaving for the present chapter, then, the second: our Lady's role in the dispensation of grace. Naturally enough—or perhaps I should say supernaturally enough—the two are interconnected; what one thinks about objective Marian co-redemption may well affect, or even determine, one's willingness to allow her a unique a role in the subsequent subjective unfolding of the economy of salvation. As John Paul II affirmed in a 1985 address at the Ecuadorian sanctuary of our Lady of Alborado, "Mary's role as co-redemptrix did not cease with the glorification of her Son."[1]

In that same chapter on co-redemption, I also made a second distinction which needs recalling in this introductory preamble to this chapter's topic. And that was a distinction between understanding Mary's co-redemptive role in terms of the incarnation only, and seeing that role as beginning with the incarnation—in effect, with the Annunciation—but continuing and climaxing in the events of the atonement, when she stood at the cross. Previously, I called that a contrast between a minimalizing and a maximalizing theology, but the more precise terms used by Neo-Scholastic writers are, rather, "remote," on the one hand, "immediate" on the other. All Catholic theologians would agree that Mary contributed remotely to the atonement by her Annunciation consent, for that consent allowed a redemptive incarnation to go forward. But it may be the case that not all Catholic theologians would agree that she contributed immediately to the atonement as the New Eve, assisting the reversal of humanity's fall by acting as the Second Adam's helpmate—even if, since the 1986 promulgation of the *Collectio Missarum de beata Maria*

---

1. John Paul II, 'Papal Address at the Sanctuary of Our Lady of Alborada in Guayaqui,' *L'Osservatore romano* 11 March 1985, cited in M. I. Miravalle, 'Mary, Coredemptrix, Mediatrix, Advocate: Foundational Presence in Divine Revelation,' in idem. (ed.), *Mary: Coredemptrix, Mediatrix, Advocate. Theological Foundations. Towards a Papal Definition?*, 266.

Virgine, those who jib at the idea of immediate contribution may occasionally feel some liturgical discomfort.

The distinction between the "remote" and the "immediate" is also relevant when looking at Mary as dispenser of grace. All Catholic theologians agree that Mary is remotely responsible for the dispensation of grace, insofar as her Annunciation consent was a necessary condition for the coming into being at the incarnation of the one "Mediator between God and men, the man Christ Jesus"—as Paul wrote to Timothy (1 Tim. 2:5). It may be the case that not all Catholic theologians agree that Mary is immediately responsible for the mediation of grace in the sense that, by a free divine choice, her post-assumption advocacy is a necessary accompaniment to the post-ascension intercessory activity before the Father of the Lord Jesus Christ, our great High Priest.

Mary's Role in the Subjective Redemption

When looking at the co-redemption, understood as Mary's contribution to the objective redemption, we saw that, in dependence on St. John's passion narrative, an impressive body of texts accumulated in the church, mainly in its Western portion, testifying to the conviction that Mary's consent at the Annunciation was renewed in a soteriologically significant way at the cross of her Son. Contrary to a quite widespread impression, the Second Vatican Council re-affirmed that conviction, which finds notable subsequent expression in the 1986 liturgical "Collection" just mentioned. Following the path of the doctrinal trajectory in those Marian liturgies, the onus of proof lies, it seems to me, on those who dispute any extension of Mary's co-redemptive role beyond its remote enactment in the angelic dialogue at Nazareth. When we now turn to the topic of Mary as mediatrix of graces, Mary's role in the subjective redemption, this is a fortiori the case, since there is an overwhelming body of textual material testifying to Mary's post-assumption role in subjective redemption, and this time it comes as much from the Christian East as it does from the Christian West.

Some Traditional Sources for the Doctrine of Mary as Mediatrix of Graces

The relevant material in which the sense of the faithful found expression comes in a wide variety of packaging. In the patristic period, the witnesses include popular sources, like the so-called Sibylline Oracles, a Christianized version of a second-century Jewish text, where we read that a time of repentance will be given men "by the hand of the pure Virgin," or in the third-century prayer *Sub tuum praesidium*, described in the second chapter in connection with the divine motherhood. It asks for the protection of the *Theotokos* in matters bearing on salvation.[2]

At a somewhat more sophisticated level, the Syrian doctor Balai, writing before the Council of Ephesus, asks that by the power of Mary's prayer, God may "bring peace to the whole earth and its inhabitants," while the title "mediatrix of all grace" is anticipated in the phrase "dispenser of all goods" used by one of the bishops at Ephesus, Theodotus of Ancyra, as well as in the fourth of eleven prayers to the Mother of God ascribed to St. Ephrem. The sixth-century Byzantine liturgical poet Romanos the Melodist, in one of his *kontakia*—short sequences in dialogue form—for the nativity has Mary say:

2. References to these and the following sources are taken from Emile Druwé, "La médiation universelle de Marie. Première partie: Marie corédemptrice du genre humain," in *Maria: Études sur la sainte Vierge*, I, ed. Manoir, 417–552.

You made me of all my race the mouth of the Glory; in me your earthly globe possesses an all-powerful protectress, a wall, and a fortress. Towards me look those expelled from the Paradise of delights.

Among the *Philotheotokoi*—the Byzantine doctors of the seventh to ninth centuries, whom we considered in the third chapter in relation to the immaculate conception—Germanus of Constantinople's second homily on the dormition includes a prayer to Mary which sets the tone for an avalanche of subsequent devotional texts:

Mary, full of kindness and compassion,
who—apart from your Son—
cares so much about mankind as you?
Who unceasingly protects us in our distress?
Who sets us free from temptation?
Who intercedes for us sinners as you do?
Who decides in our favor as you do,
when we fall into despair?
As a Mother you have
freedom and influence with your Son;
you use your intercession to save us.
Whoever was cast down
and did not turn to you?
Who has not been heard
after having called for your guidance?[3]

John Henry Newman, in his response to Pusey's *Eirenicon,* while admitting that Latin Catholic devotion to Mary was a difficulty for Anglicans and sometimes rightly so, pointed out that the Byzantine Euchologion, the equivalent of the Roman Missal, and such other liturgical books as the Triodion and the Pentekostarion, used in the Byzantine Office, hugely surpass the Missal and Breviary in the volume and amplitude of texts ascribing to Mary a continued role in human salvation.[4]

3. Germanus, *Second Homily for the Dormition* at P. G. 98, cols. 349–352
4. J. H. Newman, *Certain Difficulties Felt by Anglicans in Catholic Teaching Considered*, II., 155–164.

Newman might have mentioned, but didn't, the iconographic evidence complementing the literary data here, and notably the icon of the Mother of God of the Protecting Veil or Cloak, which shows Mary holding out the garment I mentioned at the end of the chapter on the assumption: the robe relic brought in the fifth century from Palestine to the church of the imperial palace in Constantinople. This Constantinopolitan icon-type, once transferred to the Russian context after the conversion of Kievan Rus' in the late tenth century became one of the most popular of all Marian images in Russia, the *Pokrov*. The equivalent in the medieval West is the image of our Lady's mantle, shown as a giant-sized Mary wrapping her cloak around a variety of folk diverse in ecclesial and civil status. Especially common in the later Middle Ages, its popularity survived into the early modern period when, with the invention of printing, it was often accompanied by a prayer with a form of words such as this one from an Innsbruck print of 1640:

> O mother of compassion,
> your mantle is already spread out.
> Whoever diligently places himself under it
> will not be brought low in any danger.
> Merciful patroness,
> Mary, come to our aid.
> Your mantle is so very broad and wide,
> beneath it all of Christendom can hide.
> It covers the whole wide world,
> it is our refuge and shelter.
> Merciful patroness,
> Mary, come to our aid.[5]

In the Greek and Slavonic East, the sense of Mary's spiritual motherhood of the redeemed found expression in icons notable for

---

5. Cited Caroline Ebertshäuser at al., *Mary: Art, Culture, and Religion through the Ages* (New York: Crossroad, 1998), 101.

their wonder-working powers, though of these powers, the most constant was precisely the capacity of the icons to manifest the protective care of the Mother of God in matters of salvational good. Spiritual protection was also expected from Marian images in the West: one has only to think of the devotion surrounding the black Madonnas at Czestechowa or Einsiedeln, or more widely the cult figures at the pre-Reformation East Anglian Marian shrines of Walsingham and Ipswich. But among the Marian shrines studied by two American social anthropologists in the 1980s—and incidentally, these investigators computed that at that time such centers made up at the time 66 per cent of all places of pilgrimage in modern Western Europe, it will probably not surprise us to learn that the best attended are those connected with Marian apparitions.[6] And so I want to say a word about such apparitions now. Like the Marian icons that magnetized devotion to the Mother of the faithful, and like much Marian hymnography in its concern with Mary as helper, and like the legendary material associated with Marian shrines at large, much of which is concerned with favors worked at Mary's intercession, claimed apparitions of the Blessed Virgin Mary carry a wider message pertinent to our topic.

The Place of Apparitions

Assuming for the purpose of the argument the authenticity of the major apparitions, and speaking without prejudice to the particular aims intrinsic to this or that alleged Marian intervention, the general significance of such apparitions is that they are exceptional manifestations of Mary's habitual presence: habitual presence, that is, to the life of her ecclesial children as spiritual mother of all the

6. Mary Lee Nolan and S. Nolan, *Christian Pilgrimage in Modern Western Europe* (Chapel Hill, NC: University of North Carolina Press, 1989).

redeemed. Through signs which, to the graced imagination, embody a sensuous presence of Mary, visionaries such as Bernadatte of Lourdes enjoy an exceptional but transient experience which is, though, of wider theological importance in that it recalls the permanent presence to the church, as intercessor or advocate, of the Mother of Jesus Christ.[7]

While we customarily think of Marian apparitions as typically a nineteenth- or twentieth-century Roman Catholic phenomenon,[8] the earliest example we have is known to us from St. Gregory of Nyssa's Oration on his namesake, Gregory the Wonderworker, the apostle of Cappadocia, and comes therefore from the fourth century. So far as the Christian East is concerned, in both Greek Orthodoxy and the Coptic Church separated from Rome, apparitions have been claimed in modern times, notably, in the second part of the twentieth century, on one of the Greek islands and at Cairo.

The most obvious reason why Marian apparitions have figured so highly as an expression of Mary's spiritual motherhood in the modern West lies in the emergence of new technologies of transport and communications which enable what in earlier periods were essentially localized expressions of heaven/earth interchange to be extended to the scale of mass participation. The French Mariologist René Laurentin, who has pioneered the scholarly study of the modern apparitions in multivolume editions of documents concerning, notably, La Salette, Lourdes, and Pontmain, as well as by zealous interviewing of living visionaries or alleged visionaries as at Medjugorje, argues that the global celebrity of such apparitions is misleading. The high number, in recent times, of prima facie credible

7. André Bossard, S. M. M., 'Les apparitions de Marie,' in *Kecharitôménê: Mélanges René Laurentin* (Desclée: Paris, 1990), 327–337.
8. Barbara Pope, 'Immaculate and Powerful: The Marian Revival in the Nineteenth Century,' in Clarissa W. Atkinson, Constance H. Buchanan, Margaret R. Miles (eds.), *Immaculate and Powerful: The Female in Sacred Image and Social Reality* (Boston: Beacon, 1985), 173–199.

apparitions occurring in widely separated geographical locations is, he thinks, sending a message, rather, that these words of grace are mainly intended for local consumption. They are meant for the spiritual welfare of particular individuals, groups, milieux, rather than for the edification of the church at large. One wonders, however, how far his approach—small is beautiful—fits with the content of some of the recent cases (for example, the "Mother of the hidden and mystical wounds" who allegedly appears at Surbiton with a message about the martyr status of aborted children worldwide) or how, for that matters, it fits the case of the best known early twentieth-century apparition, Fatima, which given its references to Russia and the pope, surely sought to arouse a more than local reaction.

Of course, such apparitions do not require an assent of faith from Catholics any more than do the narratives of gracious Marian action linked to icons or sanctuaries. One can take them or leave them. Possibly—and leaving aside here Pope Francis's interest in Fatima—we may be hearing rather less of them in the future, since in July 2007 the Congregation for the Doctrine of the Faith issued *monita* ("warnings") against a number of claimed apparitions, simultaneously lumping together rather disparate phenomena bothering bishops, in a way that recalls the negative policy of the Holy Office in earlier decades—the late 1940s and early 1950s—which had the effect of postponing till John Paul II's pontificate the canonization of major mystics, such as St. Faustina Kowalska of "Divine Mercy" fame. However, a solid basis in canon law for impeding the diffusion of material about new apparitions, or claimed apparitions, only really existed under the 1917 Codex of the Latin Church, the relevant canons of which were abrogated by Paul VI in response to the desire of the Second Vatican Council for the charisms and initiatives of the lay faithful to be allowed greater scope.[9] If frustrated, devotees have a tendency to become a "church of apparitions," an odd collection of disconnected groups served by disgruntled priests who harbor grievances against the official church. That could be a ground for permitting maximum liberty—or the opposite. But whatever policy is put in place, in principle Marian apparitions illustrate the claim of John Paul II in his Marian encyclical *Redemptoris Mater* that "the mediation of Mary is closely linked to her motherhood," since "with a motherly love she cooperates in the birth and education of the sons and daughters of Mother Church."[10]

"Birth" and "education" are relevant here because Marian apparitions can both convert and form. And to cite Laurentin again, this time more favorably, investigation of the common content of those apparitions the church has approved provides a useful sort of spiritual profile of the Mary of the post-assumption economy of grace. As Laurentin sums up, the common content of the modern apparitions on which church authority has looked benignly would include her youthfulness, tenderness, sorrow when speaking of sin, and smile.[11]

Conjunction of the Traditional Sources with Scripture

When we come to assess the doctrinal bearings of these various testimonies—emerging titles as in Ephrem and Theodotus of Ancyra, private prayer as with the *Sub tuum* or the Germanus homily, worshipping acts, as in the Byzantine liturgical sources enumerated by Newman, iconography as with the Pokrov or Our Lady's Mantle, miracle legends linked to shrines, or, finally, Marian apparitions, then the scriptural starting point has surely to be St. Luke's account in

9. René Laurentin, *The Apparitions of the Blessed Virgin Mary Today* (Dublin: Veritas, 1991, 2nd edition), 5.
10. John Paul II, *Redemptoris mater* 38; 44.
11. Laurentin, *The Apparitions of the Blessed Virgin Mary Today*, 34.

the Acts of the Apostles of Mary convened with the apostles in the Jerusalem Upper Room to await in expectant prayer the coming of the Pentecostal Spirit. It is by that Spirit that there is brought to earth the salvation won by the God-man on the cross, the grace of which Christ apportions as Lord and Savior by virtue of his ascension sovereignty. Edward Schillebeeckx wrote by way of commentary on Mary in the Upper Room:

> The experience of Pentecost meant . . . that her universal significance within the plan of salvation . . . became for her too an event of explicit awareness and freely accepted activity. In faith she attained at Pentecost the summit of her understanding of her true place at the very heart and centre of the young Church.[12]

With this Lukan scene in the Cenacle we then need to join up the Johannine scenario of the Mother at the victorious cross, when the Son of Man is lifted up and where she receives in the person of the beloved disciple the spiritual motherhood of the whole church.

Her role in the service of the subjective redemption is to be, so we can infer from the conjunction of these two New Testament sources, a role of intercession or advocacy, empowered by the Holy Spirit but taking the form of an exercise of ecclesial motherhood in imploring for disciples a share in the all-availing grace of salvation won by her Son.

The Attitude of the Contemporary Magisterium

John Paul II summed that up in lapidary fashion in *Redemptoris mater* when he wrote:

> Mary's motherhood continues unceasingly in the Church as the mediation which intercedes.[13]

---

12. E. Schillebeeckx, O. P., *Mary, Mother of the Redemption,* 99.

For support he could appeal to *Lumen gentium* where the fathers of the Second Vatican Council declared:

> [The] motherhood of Mary in the order of grace continues uninterruptedly from the consent which she loyally gave at the Annunciation and which she sustained without wavering beneath the Cross, until the eternal fulfillment of all the elect. Taken up to heaven, she did not lay aside this saving office but by her manifold intercession continues to bring us the gifts of eternal salvation. By her maternal charity, she cares for the brethren of her Son, who still journey on earth surrounded by dangers and difficulties, until they are led into their blessed home. Therefore the Blessed Virgin is invoked in the Church under the titles of Advocate, Helper, Benefactress, and Mediatrix.[14]

During the council sessions, the Byzantine rite Catholic bishop Vladimir Malanczuk was instrumental in ensuring that the term "mediatrix" should be retained in the schema (as with co-redemptrix, there were ecumenical anxieties about Protestant sensibilities).[15] He did so on the ground that the idea of Mary's mediation—in Greek, *mesiteia*—accentuated by specifications that bring out its preeminence and universality when compared with the intercessory activity of other saints, was essential to the integrity of the Oriental tradition. In his words:

> It appears certain from the Oriental tradition that the co-operation of the Blessed Virgin Mary in the distribution of graces, as Mother of those to be saved, is a fact; it remains a matter of free debate as a theologoumenon concerning the precise manner of Mary's mediation, for that [i. e. the precise manner] is not clear from the sources of revelation.[16]

13. John Paul II, *Redemptoris mater*, 40.

14. *Lumen gentium*, 62

15. M. O'Carroll, C. S. Sp., 'Mary, Coredemptress, Mediatress, Advocate: Instrument of Catholic-Orthodox Unity,' in Mark I. Miravalle (ed.), *Mary: Coredemptrix, Mediatrix, Advocate: Theological Foundations: Towards a Papal Definition?*, 119–143, and here at 122–124.

16. Ibid., 123–124.

As we shall see, the metropolitan was correct in saying that, among those who hold there is an immediate (not simply remote) cooperation of Mary in all subjective redemption, no complete consensus exists on the "how" as distinct from the "that." But he was also right to draw attention to the deplorable impression which would have been made on the Eastern Orthodox and other separated Orientals by any refusal of the Second Vatican Council to confirm the legitimacy of the term "mediatrix" (parallel to its refusal to sanction "co-redemptrix"). We are sometimes given the impression that all ecumenical dialogues are convergent, such that advance on one front is necessarily advance on all. To the contrary, hard choices must sometimes be made because advance in one direction can well mean regress in another. There can be no question that the major theologians of Byzantine Orthodoxy after the schism with Rome did indeed both preserve and develop a doctrine of Marian mediation of graces. They did this either in a simply christological idiom, as with Nicholas Cabasilas (died 1322) who describes Mary as "co-cause," *synaitios*, with Christ of our sanctification,[17] or in a combined christological and pneumatological vein, as with Theophanes of Nicaea (died 1381) who writes:

> The Mother of him who, through his unspeakable goodness, willed to be called our brother, is the dispenser and distributor of all the wondrous uncreated gifts of the divine Spirit, which make us Christ's brothers and co-heirs, not only because she is granting the gifts of her natural Son to his brothers in grace but also because she is bestowing them on these as her own true sons, though not by the ties of nature but of grace.[18]

Metropolitan Vladimir's intervention at Vatican II not only helped to ensure the persistence of the title "mediatrix" from the magisterium

---

17. Ibid., 137, referring to Cabasilas' homily *On the Dormition*, 13.
18. Theophanes, *Sermon on the Most Holy Godbearer*, 15, quoted in M. O'Carroll, C. S. Sp., 'Mary, Coredemptress, Mediatress, Advocate: Instrument of Catholic Orthodox Unity', art. cit., 141.

of the pre-conciliar popes, beginning with Pius IX, into that of the post-conciliar popes, notably John Paul II. It also had the further merit of pointing out that Mary's activity of *mesiteia*, "mediation," is not just another example of the intercession of the saints generally. To think so would be to undervalue the force of the early Byzantine distinction fully accepted in the pre-Reformation West, between the veneration, *doulia*, given to the saints at large, and special version of that veneration, called *hyperdoulia*, given to the Mother of God. To be sure, Marian mediation belongs with the article of the Creed which confesses the *communio sanctorum*, the co-sharing of holy gifts by holy persons in the church on the basis of the economies of the Son and the Spirit. But Marian mediation cannot be understood by reference simply to the mode of operation of the communion of saints generally conceived. There is a distinguishing factor which makes her role in the communication of the fruits of the objective redemption more specific—indeed, unique. And it is in the description of that factor, and its conditions of working, that the task and the difficulty of a theology of Marian mediation consists.

Is Marian Mediation Universal?

One key word the bishop noted in this connection was "universal" though the question soon arises of the nature and limits of the universality concerned. The basic thesis was known to the medieval Latin doctors. For Bernard in his homily on the nativity of Mary, Christ is the fount of life, Mary the aqueduct for the same waters, such that—switching metaphors in a homily for the Vigil of the Lord's Nativity—God willed that we should have nothing that did not pass through the hands of Mary. These two metaphors—aqueduct or channel and hands—recur in the Franciscan doctor Bernardine of Siena and in the influential *Mariale* ascribed to St. Albert which also condenses them into a conceptual formula. Mary's role is to be "distributive of all goods [in the salvific order] *universaliter*," "universally." This was a widespread—not to say, the common—teaching of theologians up to the mid-eighteenth century when some Catholic writers, more or less under Enlightenment inspiration, began to draw back from it and to treat it as a pious exaggeration. That was so in the case of the historian of the ancient church Luigi Antonio Muratori in his 1747 treatise *Della regolata devozione dei cristiani* to which three years later Alphonsus Liguori published a reply in his *Le glorie de Maria*, "The Glories of Mary." Translated into various languages, St. Alphonsus's book was to become a nineteenth-century bestseller, though, as we know, *vox populi* is not always *vox Dei*.

Muratori's scepticism, Newman's admission to Pusey of horror at some of the rhetorical excesses in Mariological writing, and even, more recently, the philo-Protestant proclivities, if such they were, of influential *periti* at the Second Vatican Council, played a valuable role in obliging Catholic theologians to speak with more nuance about the universality of Marian mediation, or at least to draw out its nature with more clarity.

Thus for example, the Toulouse Dominican Marie-Joseph Nicolas in his "Essai de synthèse mariale," insisted that Mary acts by her prayer which, while it is certain to be heard, has no strict *right* to be heard, in which latter respect it differs from the prayer as man of the glorified Christ. Moreover, her certainty of being heard is entirely conditioned by her uniting her own prayer to that of Christ. This leads Nicolas to his key formulation which runs:

> These two wills [Mary's and the human will of Christ] that together make only one and of which [Mary's] is entirely prayer [i. e. request],

while [Christ's] is a true demand, determine by their accord, which moreover is inevitable, the gift of all graces.[19]

Mary's merciful intercession, so exercised, is itself a deliberate disposition on the part of Christ, the Son. Christ, so Nicolas writes, "arrang[ed] for this Advocate [Mary] so as to make us appreciate by the idea and image of this woman who has about her nothing of the judge, his own will to pardon and save us." [20]

Those words read like an exculpatory commentary on the early nineteenth-century Marian appearance at La Salette, whose message was often interpreted along the lines of "Mary, mercy; Jesus, justice": a contrast carefully avoided in Nicolas's formulation. And Nicolas goes on to comment on the two most common titles of Mary as heavenly mediatrix: namely, "mother" on the one hand and "queen" on the other. He proposes that Mary's mediatorial action can be called "motherly" from the sentiments which animate it and by its proper effect—the birth and growth of human beings in the divine life, and it can also be called "queenly" in that it enjoys an all-powerful moral authority with the King, Jesus Christ.

The question of moral authority raises the issue of the mode of causality which Marian intercession entails. On Nicolas's theology of Mary's queenly mediation, this would be moral causality, and this is surely preferable to speaking of a physical causality as with the sacraments—the other standard reference point in talk of mediation by created secondary causes of saving grace. On the Thomist view, strongly represented as this in Catholic theology, the sacraments are efficient instrumental causes of grace because by their nature—physically, then—they are themselves acts of the divine Word who can make himself effectively present or active wherever he

19. Marie-Joseph Nicolas, "Essai de synthèse mariale," *Maria: Études sur la Sainte Vierge* I, ed. Manoir, 707–741, and here at 737.
20. Ibid., 738.

choose. To ascribe physical causality to Mary's prayers would seem to imply that Mary's mode of existence or the range of her activity is now ubiquitous in a way that can be compared with that of Christ who in his divine hypostasis is God the Word. But this does not form part of Catholic discourse except in such playful conceits as the poem by the Victorian Jesuit Gerard Manley Hopkins, "The Blessed Virgin Mary Compared to the Air We Breathe."

Speaking of sacraments brings me to what is probably the chief qualification a sane account of Marian mediation ought to include. The formula "mediatrix of all graces" reads as though it ought to include sacramental graces as well, but the identity of sacramental acts as acts of the incarnate Word who, in his human nature, is our great High Priest militates against a Marian moment in sacramental engracing *as such*. The French Jesuit Edouard Druwé, writing like Nicolas in the first volume of *Maria*, a comprehensive eight-volume collection whose publication spans the years from the eve of the dogmatization of the assumption to the close of the Second Vatican Council, remarks helpfully on this topic:

> The order of the subjective redemption [is] the totality of the conditions which place human beings within the irradiation of the redemptive mystery *already present in the Church by the sacraments*.[21]

In other words, our Lady's contribution to subjective redemption presupposes the sacraments and their intrinsic efficacy as already in place. The universality of Mary's motherly intercession—thus Druwé—is related to the sacraments only in what concerns those providential arrangements and actual graces which render us receptive to occasions of sacramental grace and so make that grace more fruitful in our lives. In those ways there can be a Marian

---

21. Druwé, "La médiation universelle de Marie," in *Maria: Études sur la sainte Vierge* I, ed. Manoir, 417–452, and here at 561. Emphasis is added.

moment in sacramental living—but only in those indirect senses can one speak of a Marian moment in relation to sacramental grace as such.

To give an example, a man goes on a Mediterranean cruise and finds he is sharing his cabin with a priest (providential arrangement). On impulse (actual grace) he makes a sacramental confession, something he has not done for forty years. That is the field of play for Marian mediation, not the sacrament of penance as such. So to call Mary "mediatrix of graces" is preferable—where her immediate, as distinct from remote, role in subjective redemption is concerned, to calling Mary "mediatrix of *all* grace," or graces as such. Evidently, the role accorded on this view to Marian intercession remains ample; her prayer activity on our behalf is such as to be comparable, in Hopkins' words, to the "air we breathe"—and such "air" can be not only a sweet breeze but also devastatingly powerful.[22]

In the late 1920s, the founder of the higher Institute of Scholastic Thought at Louvain, Cardinal Mercier, commissioned an Orientalist who was also a competent Neo-Scholastic dogmatic theologian, Joseph-Martin Lebon, to compose an office and mass for our Lady Mediatrix of All Grace—originally for the archdiocese of Malines-Brussels though in 1931 this was extended to all Belgium and indeed, at the behest of Pius XI, to any diocese of the Latin Church that wished to use it. In "The Apostolicity of the Doctrine of Marian Mediation," Lebon explained the rationale of his texts. [23] For him the scope of Marian mediation included co-redemption as well as the mediation of grace, but what fused together his account of both

---

22. As in Edward Booth's unpublished poem, "Mary the displacing air," where she is compared more to storm than to zephyr. "The vastness of the travelling air is gigantic, for/ meteora at all its levels are moved, displaced. . . . Why not a sign of Mary's power?" Text communicated to the present writer on April 29, 2013.

23. Joseph Lebon, "L'apostolicité de la docrine de la médiation mariale," *Recherches de théologie ancienne et médiévale* 2 (1930): 129–159.

aspects of Mary's role was his claim, based on a trio of ante-Nicene authors, Justin, Irenaeus, and Tertullian,[24] that Mary is associated with Christ in what Lebon called a "total principle of restoration and salvation." Because her role in this "total principle of restoration and salvation" is, as he put it, "official and ordinary," it is clearly distinguished from that of other saints. In a subsequent essay,[25] and against this New Eve background, Lebon argued that while it made sense to hold that Mary is located within the service of the achieved work of the Redeemer, more fundamentally her place as intermediary of salvation is not between the Redeemer and those already redeemed by him, but with the Redeemer in his saving action, and thus between the triune God and the estranged humanity which awaits reconciliation and redemption.[26]

The liturgical texts Lebon devised, which can be found in the 1962 Missal and the last editions of the pre-1974 breviary were, however, altered in crucial regards by Pius XI. The pope changed the wording of the collect which in Lebon's original opened, "Almighty and eternal God" so that now it was addressed instead to Christ. He also altered the form of the invitatory antiphon at matins which had read, "Let us worship almighty God who wanted us to have all good things through Mary" so that it began instead, "Let us worship Christ the Redeemer." Lebon was not pleased. What now had become of the total conjoint christological-Mariological principle of restoration and salvation? But the deed was done before he had a chance (as he says) to explain his thinking to the pope.

So far as the theology of co-redemption is concerned, Lebon was right to situate Mary with Christ between the Trinity and ourselves

24. Lebon was keen on the links between the first two figures, notably Irenaeus, with the "presbyters of Asia" and thus with Polycarp and in that way with the apostle John.
25. Idem., "Comme je conçois, j'établis et je défende la doctrine de la mediation mariale," *Ephemerides theologicae lovanienses* 16 (1939): 655–744.
26. Ibid., 665.

for the New Eve typology demands this, but too the pope's instinct was also sound when he restructured this scheme for the post-assumption mediation of graces, thus resituating Mary in this second regard between Christ and ourselves, for the historic symbolism of aqueduct and hands as found in the Latin divines suggests this. Acting as guardian of the Liturgy Pius XI thus added a caesura, though not an outright separation, between these two aspects of Mary's contribution to the world's salvation. It would then fall to the speculative theologian to explain in terms of principles and not just historical references why a different scheme is appropriate for each of the two aspects of Mary's role in redemption.

In any case, so long as the co-redemption is retained as a contribution to the objective redemption, the notion of a joint christological-Mariological principle of salvation remains intact. In the words of the Anglo-Catholic theologian Eric Mascall, the Mother of God was and is "*within* [his emphasis] the redemptive act."[27] If so, that will necessarily have implications for the structure of the church which flows from the redemptive act as the human sphere where salvation is accessible. It's the theme of our Lady and the church we shall be looking at in the chapter that follows.

27. E. L. Mascall, *Corpus Christi: Essays on the Church and the Eucharist*, 2nd ed. (London, UK: Dacre Press, 1965), 95.

7

Our Lady and the Church

We saw in the fifth chapter how, among Neo-Scholastics, the background to the dogmatization of the assumption lay in heavy reliance on the ability of dogmatic theology to deduce, or at least infer, the various Marian privileges from each other. This was possible because all of these privileges—from divine motherhood and perpetual virginity through immaculate conception and co-redemption to assumption—could be regarded as interlinked by ties of either necessity (hence "deduce") or fittingness, *convenientia* (hence "infer"). I suggested that, in some cases at least, such Neo-Scholastic theologians were not especially interested in historical facts, the close examination of the sources of revelation in Scripture and tradition, which on a more satisfactory view of theology, such as I outlined in the opening chapter, takes precedence, methodologically speaking, over systematic construction in dogmatic thought.

The Rise of "Ecclesio-typical" Mariology

Paradoxically, the same period—the 1940s and 50s—was also characterized by the rise to fame and fortune of a kind of Mariology which used the demand for more attention to biblical and traditional—meaning, above all, patristic—sources to challenge the Marian thinking found in the Latin Church since the Catholic Reformation, of which the Neo-Scholastic Mariological style was itself one variant. The movements of biblical and patristic *ressourcement* threw up a new (or was it, rather, very old?) kind of Mariology which soon acquired the nickname of "ecclesio-typical," over against, "christo-typical," Mariology. In other words, this was to be a type of reflection which linked Mary not so much to Christ—which had been the case in all early modern and modern Mariology hitherto—as to the church, or, to put this more sympathetically, linked Mary to Christ only in, with, and through the church, the messianic people, prepared in the Old Testament, launched on its great adventure in the New. As we shall see, the tension between christo-typical and ecclesio-typical Mariologies hardened into outright conflict at the time of the Second Vatican Council.

Conflict at the Second Vatican Council

Such conflict might have been expected because the two Mariologies gave very different answers to the question, 'What is the primary or fundamental principle of all Mariology?," a question put in that form as early as the middle 1930s. But the sharpening of tension between christo-typical and ecclesio-typical Mariologies set the fathers of the Second Vatican Council at loggerheads for another reason too. The question of whether one should take as one's starting-point Mary and the church, or, alternatively, Mary and Jesus Christ, became entangled with another and quite different question: namely, whether in Catholic belief and practice the Marian element should be minimalized or maximalized, and indeed whether one's attitude to the de facto Marian patrimony in the church should be, in a vocabulary suggested by René Laurentin, "critical" or, alternatively, "mystical" (for which latter term he also proposed as a quasi-synonym, "devout").[1]

Thus several somewhat ill-assorted enquiries came to be lumped together. First, does the evidence of Scripture and the Fathers indicate that Mary's relation to the church is more constitutive of her theological significance than is her relation to Christ? Second, should Mariology have one single primary or fundamental principle, governing all the rest? Third, had Marianism in the Catholic Church gone too far and, for pastoral reasons, of which the most obvious was the demands of ecumenical convergence with separated Christians, did it need to be cut back? Fourth and lastly, what was the proper epistemic mode in which to practice Mariology? Was it an objective mode of knowledge, concerned as far as possible to treat the textual evidence neutrally, or at least coolly, with the professional historian's sobriety, or should it be, rather, by an engaged mode of knowledge which looked at the same evidence in the light of the wider conviction that the Mother of the Redeemer had always been spiritually present to the faithful and continues to be so today.

Once one distinguishes out these four enquiries it becomes obvious, or so it seems to me, that what alarmed the more conservative bishops and theological advisers at Vatican II was not the theme of "our Lady and the church" as such (how could that be threatening in itself?), but the combining of all four issues into

---

1. René Laurentin, "Un problème initial de méthodologie mariale," in *Maria: Études sur la sainte Vierge*, I, ed. Manoir, 697–706.

a synthetic whole of a distinctive kind. One synthetic combination of the four could run as follows: the ecclesio-typical approach, predominant in Bible and Fathers, is itself the fundamental governing principle of all Mariology, on whose basis Mariology should be practiced minimalizingly, and in a critical epistemic mode. This was the synthesis, or to put it less flatteringly the cocktail of opinions, which produced the low Mariology of the later 1960s and 70s, itself extended through Liberation Theology into the 1980s. Mary of Nazareth is sublime chiefly as a representative of the faith (or, in Liberationism, the hope) of the wider church.[2] In reality, however, the four issues I enumerated are perfectly separable. The ingredients of the cocktail can be separated out as in a fruit cocktail rather than the sort of cocktail served at a bar.

Ressourcement Writers on "Our Lady and the Church"

After these largely introductory remarks, let me then embark on a brief review of what theologians of biblical and patristic *ressourcement* had to say about the theme of "our Lady and the church." I give four examples of such writers.

In the revival of Catholic Scripture scholarship in France Lucien Deiss, who was better known after the Second Vatican Council for his biblically inspired liturgical music, had combined an historical approach to the mystery of salvation with a retrieval of biblical typology, understanding the latter as the key to the literary structure of the Scriptures that witness to that mystery. In so doing, Deiss aimed to show that Mary was, in a celebrated phrase, "the church before the church," *l'Église avant l'Église*.[3] In other words, our Lady

2. Wolfgang Beinert, "Himmelskönigin – Urbild der Kirche – neue Frau. Die Wandlungen des katholischen Marienbildes von der Gegenreformation bis zum Ende des 20," in *Maria: Eine ökumenische Herausforderung,* ed. Beinert (Regensburg: Pustet, 1984), 75–116.

was the climactic spiritual ending of the chosen people of the Old Covenant and at the same time the beginning of the reconfiguration of that people in the New. In her own person she was the passage between the Old and New Testaments. She was the church—but before its deployment in the faith and hierarchical organization of the apostolic mission. Here was typological fulfillment since in Mary, the personification of Israel as the daughter of Zion of the prophetic books or the bride of the Song of Songs in the Wisdom literature at last received full expression in flesh and blood reality.

Predictably, exegetes like Deiss made much of the bifocal quality—at once Marian and ecclesial—of the Woman clothed with the Sun in Apocalypse 12. They found that the intercessory role of Mary at Cana in the second chapter of St. John's Gospel recalls the function of the praying church. They meditated on Mary's role as mother of believers in the Johannine passion narrative. The "Israel according to the Spirit" whom Christ wedded to himself on the cross according to Ephesians 5 is, they said, embodied in the New Eve of the church personified in Mary, an echo of whose wedding with the Redeemer resounds in Paul's betrothing the Corinthian church to Christ—thus 2 Cor. 11:2, "a pure bride to her one husband."

Some of this exegesis was itself indebted to patristic commentary, but the chief patrologists who contributed to the emergence of ecclesio-typical Mariology were German-speaking, not French. The fundamental reference point was the Swiss German Alois Müller, my second *ressourcement* theologian, in his study *Ecclesia-Maria*, "Church-Mary" (in English that would sound better as "Mary-Church"), the explanatory subtitle of which was "The Unity of Mary and the Church."[4] Confining himself to the Fathers of the age before

---

3. Lucien Deiss, *Marie, fille de Sion* (Paris: Desclée de Brouwer, 1959).

4. Alois Müller, *Ecclesia-Maria: Die Einheit Marias und der Kirche* (Freiburg in der Schweiz: Universitätsverlag, 1951; 1955, 2nd ed.).

the Council of Ephesus, Müller found that patristic ecclesiology asserted both the virginity of the church, identified with the purity of the church's faith, and the motherhood of the church, itself linked with the church's bridal character, by which motherhood the church as the spouse of Christ brings her children to birth in faith by means of the waters of baptism. These two interrelated features—virginity and motherhood, especially bridal motherhood—evidently recall (whatever we are to make of this fact) the virgin mother of Jesus. In some sense, then, for major players in the ante-Ephesian epoch, the virginal motherhood of the church began in Mary.

Who were the Fathers to whom Müller appealed? Among the Western writers before Ephesus a trio can be singled out. The North African Tertullian, in the treatise *On the Flesh of Christ*, saw the New Eve as both Mary and the church. Ambrose of Milan, in the little book *On the Institution of Virgins*, says that virgins are called to imitate at once Mary and the church: they should meditate on the beautiful mysteries prophesied of Mary as figure of the church. Furthermore, in his commentary on the Gospel of Luke, Ambrose maintains it is because Mary is the type of the church that she had to remain forever a virgin. As for Augustine, with whom Müller's survey of the Latin Fathers ends (he died in 429, the year before the council was summoned), whereas the bishop of Hippo can refer to Mary minimalizingly as one of the church's members, he also calls her "truly the mother of [Christ's members] which we are."[5]

Where the Orientals are concerned, one name will have to suffice, that of St. Ephrem, the most graphic of Müller's witnesses, since he gives the church the title "Mary" as well as calling both Mary and the church spouse, mother, and daughter of the divine Son (though, as with all references to Ephrem by non-specialists, some caution

5. Augustine, *De sancta virginitate*, 6.

about authorship is necessary since so many texts in early Syrian Christianity were transmitted under his name).

If Müller put down the torch at Ephesus, it was taken up again, so far as the Western patristic tradition was concerned, by a third *ressourcement* Mariologist, Leo Scheffczyk, a Silesian made cardinal for his services to theology by John Paul II. In contrast to Müller, Scheffczyk did not choose to introduce the parallel between Mary and the church into the actual title of his key work, and yet he makes it plain that "the mystery of Mary in the piety and teaching of the Carolingian age" (the name of his ground-breaking study), includes very importantly the self-same parallelism: Mary-church.[6]

Thus for example, among the authors Scheffczyk discusses, the black monk Paschasius Radbert in a commentary on the Gospel according to Matthew, had described Mary as prefiguring and preparing the church which, by Mary, is united to the Bridegroom, while a sermon on the assumption ascribed to another Carolingian figure, Ildephonsus of Toledo, asserts that all the goods diffused in the church are spread abroad from a starting point in Mary.

These investigations by German-speaking theologians—Müller, Scheffczyk—into the ecclesio-typical bearings of patristic texts about Mary stimulated the publication in Rome in 1954 of a study drawn from an otherwise unnoticed thesis from the year of the outbreak of war, 1939, on the Mary/church parallel in the Latin tradition till the end of the twelfth century.[7] The Breton Jesuit Hervé Coathalem—fourth and last of my quartet—after completing his doctoral work, sank into comparative obscurity in Jesuit Universities in the Philippines and Vietnam. Before doing so, Coathalem had been able to show how the Marian ideas of the Carolingian divines

---

6. Leo Scheffczyk, *Das Mariengeheimnis in Frömmigkeit und Lehre der Karolingerzeit* (Leipzig: St. Benno-Verlag, 1959).

7. Hervé Coathalem, *Le parallelisme entre la sainte Vierge et l'église dans la tradition Latine jusqu'a la fin du XIIe siècle* (Rome: Analecta Gregoriana, 1954).

passed into the immediately pre-Scholastic authors of the eleventh and twelfth centuries. In these writers, so Coathalem showed, it is a commonplace that the church is mirrored in Mary and Mary in the church—the church, that is, as Holy Mother Church, the virgin bride of Christ. A particularly fine example of this reciprocal figuration idea—two realities mirroring each other—is found in the English Cistercian Isaac of Stella's fifty-first Sermon, of which the key section is included in the Office of Readings of the 1974 Roman Liturgy of the Hours.[8]

So the Mary-church theme continued to sound. On the eve of High Scholasticism the canon regular Godfrey of St. Victor describes the church as reborn from Christ's opened side on the cross—emphasizing "rebirth," rather than simply "birth"—since, he affirms, the church's original birth was in Mary, whom Godfrey calls *prima Ecclesiae persona*, the "first person of the Church."[9] Or again—by now we are in the thirteenth century—an early Franciscan writer, Conrad of Saxony, who in his "Mirror of the Blessed Virgin Mary," in trying to explain this ecclesial priority of our Lady, asserts that Mary holds in plenitude the ecclesial perfection distributed out in more partial ways to the saints.[10]

Why, then, we might well ask, did the high Scholastics—Thomas, Albert, Bonaventure and the rest—fail to integrate the theme *Ecclesia-Maria* into their systematic work? One suggestion runs: the orchestration of that theme was too dependent on images to be readily translated into the formal language of the schools. That is plausible, and yet it is hardly true of Conrad's doctrine just cited.

---

8. For the Second Sunday of Advent in *The Divine Office: The Liturgy of the Hours according to the Roman Rite, I* (London: Collins, 1974), 94–96.

9. Godfrey of St. Victor, *In nativitate beatae Mariae*, cited Gérard Philips, "Marie et l'Église. Un thème théologique renouvelé," in *Maria: Études sur la sainte Vierge*, VII, ed. Manoir, 363–420, and here at p. 391.

10. Conrad of Saxony, *Speculum beate Mariae Virginis* 7, cited Philips, art. cit., 389.

Whatever the reason, the Mary-church motif finds expression chiefly in the lyrical devotional texts of the high Middle Ages, texts contemporary with the great Scholastic Sentence commentaries and summas but altogether independent of them. A rightly celebrated example is Francis of Assisi's *Salutatio beatae Mariae virginis* which opens: "Hail, o Lady, holy Queen,/ holy Mother of God, Mary,/ who are the Virgin made Church."[11] The grammatical form of "the Virgin made Church," *virgo ecclesia facta*, reflects, we can note, the christological confession of the Johannine Prologue as rendered in the Latin Bible and Liturgy: *Verbum caro factum*, "the Word made flesh." And Francis's salutation continues in praise of this "Virgin made Church": "[You, Mary] in whom were and are/ all the fullness of grace and every good."

In these biblical, patristic, and post-patristic references we have a perfectly adequate legitimation for writing Mariology ecclesio-typically, at any rate in the sense of writing a Mariology that makes the motif of Mary's relation to the church one of its key themes. Notice, however, that the movements of biblical and patristic *ressourcement*—to which I've added elements of a "going back to the sources" of medieval Christianity of a kind little appealed to in Neo-Scholasticism—do not necessarily require us to say that the *Ecclesia-Maria* theme is the *dominant* theme of the Mariology of the first millennium and beyond. They only indicate it is *one* major theme. And this is hardly a controversial claim.

Enthusiasts for this theme may sometimes wish, of course, to assert its predominance in this or that writer, which is fair enough. To assert its predominance, over against all other Mariological approaches, in both Scripture and the tradition of the first ten or twelve centuries, would be, however, far more disputable, not least because of the

---

11. For this *Salutatio beatae Mariae virginis* see François d'Assise, *Écrits* (Paris: Cerf, 1981), 274.

sheer quantity of texts involved (liturgical and epigraphical as well as in the various literary genres used by the Fathers and medievals, not to mention the iconographic sources). But even a successful assertion of the predominant role of an ecclesio-typical Mariology in the tradition at large would not lead to the total supplanting of a complementary christo-typical Mariology, unless that assertion were combined with the claim that ecclesio-typicality constitutes the primary or fundamental principle of all Mariological thinking which—by definition, then—must govern systematically (comprehensively, exclusively) all authentic Marian discourse. I turn now to the question of a fundamental principle for Mariology.

A Fundamental Principle for Mariology?

As I mentioned, discussion of a fundamental first principle in Mariology dates from the 1930s. Initially, that discussion took place in the context of the christo-typical Mariologies which had set the tone in Latin Catholicism since the early seventeenth century when what were in effect distinct Scholastic tractates on Mariology began to be written. I said in the second chapter, on the divine motherhood, that Mariology as a distinct project within the wider theological enterprise is generally credited to the Baroque Scholastics, and the chief name to stress here would be the Spaniard Francisco Suárez, the outstanding Scholastic theologian of the Jesuit Society.[12] Suárez's Mariology derives entirely from the doctrine of the divine motherhood, and in this it forms the culmination of a line that runs from Cyril of Alexandria through Thomas Aquinas. The inauguration of a quite explicit debate over a fundamental first

12. For his 1585 *Quaestiones de Beata Virgine Maria* he is the hero of Sarah Jane Boss's critique of modern Mariology in her "Mary at the Margins: Christology and Ecclesiology in Modernity," *The Month* CCLVII. 1548 (December 1996): 463–475.

principle for Mariology came about through the work of a German theologian seeking to revive Suarezian clarity as to the primacy of divine motherhood in a Mariological culture where christo-typicalism was taking a variety of forms.

This was the Cologne seminary professor Carl Feckes (1894–1958), co-founder of the *Deutsche Arbeitsgemeinschaft für Mariologie*, and well-known in the German Catholicism of his time as the disciple and continuator of the nineteenth century dogmatician Matthias Joseph Scheeben, the outstanding modern German Catholic theologian till he was displaced by Karl Rahner in the 1960s. In his 1935 essay, "Das Fundamentalprinzip der Mariologie," expanded twenty years later into book form under the same title, Feckes took the view that any choice of a fundamental principle that is *not* the divine motherhood would, in his words, "violate the direction sanctioned by all tradition."[13] The discussion thus opened up continued throughout the next thirty years, though never more polemically so than in Rome, behind the scenes, as well as in the aula, at the Second Vatican Council. Feckes would hardly have been pleased had he seen the consequences of his intervention, since the shift in favour of some version of ecclesio-typicalism as the correct answer to the question, "How should we identify Mariology's fundamental principle?," went against the deepest grain of his own convictions.

That is not to say that he in any way opposed the reintroduction into Mariology of the theme of our Lady and the church as such. Not at all, since the influential Mariological section of the dogmatics of his master, Scheeben, had itself described Mary's divine motherhood as essentially a 'bridal motherhood' (*Brautmutterschaft*)—which we

---

13. Carl Feckes, "Das Fundamentalprinzip der Mariologie. Ein Beitrag zu ihrem organischen Aufbau," in *Scientia sacra: Festschrift für Kardinal Schulte* (Cologne-Dusseldorf: J. P. Bachem, 1935), 266.

can term a christo-typical Mariological concept heavy with ecclesial implications.[14] This mother, Mary, had been chosen by her Son to be his *socia*, his intimate companion and, in that sense, his bride. Participation in that relation of Mary to Christ was, for Scheeben, the key to understanding how the church too is both bride of Christ and mother of Christians, who are the body of Christ. But Scheeben, unlike Feckes, had never sought a Mariological *Fundamentalprinzip.* And so, again unlike Feckes, Scheeben had not opened a Pandora's Box from which any axiom claiming to be the all-important super-axiom could at any moment fly out.

An Ecclesio-typical Fundamental Principle in Mariology

By the 1950s, the favored opinion in a Catholic theology which considered itself to have profited by the biblical, patristic, and to a lesser degree medieval but non-Scholastic "returns to the sources" was to seek Feckes' primary principle not in divine motherhood which would, of course, imply a christo-typical Mariology, or even, for that matter in divine bridal motherhood, which would imply a christo-typical Mariology open to its ecclesio-typical counterpart, but, rather, in an ecclesio-typical Mariology *tout court.*

An attentive observer could have noted two straws to show the way the wind was blowing in 1955, which, coincidentally, was when the full length version of Feckes' 1935 essay was published, just three years before his death. The first straw in the wind was the fifth, Mariological volume, of the influential *Katholische Dogmatik* of Michael Schmaus, teacher and troublesome examiner of a certain Joseph Ratzinger.[15] In that volume, Schmaus announced his

14. Matthew Joseph Scheeben, *Mariology* (St. Louis, MO: Herder, 1947), 2 vols.; see on the point at issue, Ivo Muser, *Das mariologische Prinzip "gottesbräutliche Mutterschaft" und das Verständnis der Kirche bei M. J. Scheeben* (Rome: Analecta Gregoriana, 1995).

conversion to the ecclesio-typical axiom, "Mary is the type of the church," taken now to be the sole primary or fundamental principle of Mariology. Indeed, Schmaus went so far as to say that, while Mary's status as the type of the church cannot be deduced from her divine motherhood, the divine motherhood *can* be deduced from her status as type of the church—a claim which drew from a startled Thomistic reviewer the following vigorous comment:

> To move to an historical event [i.e. Mary's motherhood of Jesus] from a result obtained by a speculative route [i.e. from Mary's motherhood of the Church presents a difficulty that is quasi-unsurmountable.[16]

The reviewer was asking, How can an historical fact (Mary is the Mother of Jesus) be deduced from a typological assertion?

The second straw in the wind from 1955 was the French Redemptorist Clément Dillenschneider's study *Le principe premier d'une théologie mariale organique* where the author, after half a lifetime of work in a christotypical manner on our Lady's co-redemptive role, now rejected the claims to primary principle status of the divine motherhood, including its Scheebenesque "bridal motherhood" version, and plumped instead for a primary principle based on what he called "messianic motherhood," a principle which envisaged Mary as mother of the Messiah in his people.[17] This formulation, Dillenschneider thought, would bring out well the bearing of Mary's motherhood on the wider church.

15. Michael Schmaus, *Katholische Dogmatik V. Mariologie* (Munich: Hueber, 1955).
16. Albert Patfoort, "Bulletin de théologie dogmatique. Mariologie," *Revue des sciences philosophiques et théologiques* 41 (1957): 548.
17. Clément Dillenschneider, *Le principe premier d'une théologie mariale organique: Orientations* (Paris: Alsatia, 1955).

But Is a Fundamental Mariological Principle Necessary?

This starting-point could well produce a rich Mariology but the question raised by the Dominican Albert Patfoort in an essay stimulated by Dillenschenider's book was whether in Mariology (or in any other area of dogmatics for that matter) we need to look for, as he put it, a "unique principle which would permit us to deduce by a rigorous inference the totality of one or another mystery." Thinking more especially of Mariology, would, he asked, the lack of such a principle obliges us to "conclude to the absence of genuine necessities and close connexions in the mystery of Mary."[18]

Patfoort distinguished between two theological methods. One, which he ascribes to St. Thomas, highlights the inner organization of the data of revelation by identifying those particular data that represent some foundational aspect of the logic of the divine plan and then going to on to attach other data thereto. The other opposed theological method, characteristic of a hyper- systematic Neo-Scholasticism, tries to submit all revealed assertions to the hegemony of a single principle, posed once for all, from which the many revealed assertions must then be deduced.

There is, wrote Patfoort, no a priori reason why there should not be in Mariology two—let us say—primary principles, each of them supreme in what he called a given "register" or on a given "line." To explain this point he drew a comparison with the situation in Christology. In Christology, Christmas (the incarnation) and Easter (the redemption) are each primary in a certain respect. They generate, then, two coequal primary principles. Could not something similar be true in Mariology? The primacy of the divine motherhood seen as a primary christo-typical principle indicating the functions

18. Albert Patfoort, "Le principe premier de la Mariologie," *Revue des sciences philosophiques et théologiques* 41 (1957): 448.

and perfections Mary would develop thanks to her unique bond with the Word incarnate, could coexist with a second primary principle, based on the Mary-church idea. For the latter, Mary embodies the Word's reception by a wider humanity; she is the sign and prototype of the church, so this second, ecclesio-typical, primary principle shows how the functions and perfections of Mary, identified with the help of the first, christo-typical, primary principle find their expression in the fullness of influence she possesses in the mystical body of Christ, the church. Having two coequal primary principles might be thought to diminish the unity of Mariology, but in fact it contributes to the organic quality of that very unity. Obsession with locating one single fundamental primary principle was likely to lead, thought Patfoort, to a constricting of the Mariological realm, with regrettable results.[19]

The Excellence of Mary/Church Thinking

The criticisms that can justly be made of choosing an ecclesio-Marian axiom as the *sole* governing principle of Mariology should not blind us, however, to the qualities of the dogmatic thinking to which emphasis on the Mary/church relation can lead. That was strikingly shown by the finest of the German presentations, which came from the hand of Otto Semmelroth, professor of dogma at the Jesuit College of Philosophy and Theology in Frankfurt. Semmelroth's 1949 study "Archetype of the Church. The Organic Construction of the Mystery of Mary," proves conclusively, I believe, that ecclesio-typicalism does not necessarily lead to a low Mariology.[20]

19. A fuller account of these debates than can be offered here is found in Jan Radkiewicz, *Auf der Suche nach einem mariologischen Grundprinzip: Eine historische-systematische Untersuchung über die letzten hundert Jahre* (Konstanz: Hartung-Gorre, 1989).

How does it prove that? In the last chapter, on Mary as mediatrix of graces, we saw how scholastically trained theologians working in a christo-typical idiom in the French Catholicism of this period drew back from the assertion that sacramental graces—as distinct from "providential arrangements" and "actual" graces—are given through the mediation of Mary. By contrast, Semmelroth has absolutely no difficulty at all with the claim that grace in every mode, including the sacramental, is communicated through our Lady. This is because he understands Mary to be, as the primal church, the total recipient, in a single all-encompassing act of acceptance, of all the spiritual good the Savior has to give to the world.

As Semmelroth writes, "the Mother of the Lord is 'the depository for the plenitude of all graces for the Church.'"[21]

> Christ stands before the Father living on "ever to make intercession on our behalf" (Hebrews 7:25), or to use the idiom of piety, showing his wounds to the Father. Mary stands as the perpetual Orante [the praying person] in the eternally changeless attitude of the Church's receptivity before Christ, and she receives what the Church needs.[22]

Since she receives whatever the church needs she can be called, in Semmelroth's formula, the 'receptive co-redeemer.'"[23]

---

20. Otto Semmelroth, *Mary, Archetype of the Church* (Dublin: Gill, 1964). The German original of Semmelroth's book was published as early as 1949, yet fifteen years later Laurentin could write as though minimalist Mariology may be equated with ecclesio-typicality: thus his *La Question mariale* (Paris: Éditions du Seuil, 1963). Laurentin's personal position, however, wisely sought to combine the strengths of both approaches, ibid., 101–102. Hence the maxim, "wholly correlative to Christ, wholly correlative to the Church," adopted (in a slightly modified wording) by the present writer in *Epiphany: A Theological Introduction to Catholicism* (Collegeville, MN: Liturgical Press, 1996), 338.
21. Semmelroth, *Mary, Archetype of the Church*, 106.
22. Ibid. His study retains a place of honor in the book of essays co-written in the 1980s by Pope Benedict XVI and Hans Urs von Balthasar, on the same theme: H. U. von Balthasar and J. Ratzinger, *Maria—Kirche im Ursprung*, 4th ed. (Einsiedeln: Johannes Verlag, 1997); the English translation is *Mary: The Church at the Source*, trans. Adrian Walker (San Francisco: Ignatius Press, 2005).
23. Semmelroth, *Mary, Archetype of the Church*, 106.

These formulations demonstrate that an ecclesio-typical Mariology, even if practiced to the exclusion of a christo-typical Mariology and acknowledging its own inner principle as the sole fundamental axiom (as is the case with Semmelroth) does not *necessarily* lead to Mariological minimalism, *pace* certain anxieties expressed at, and after, Vatican Council II.

At the Second Vatican Council

I move back now in conclusion to the scene at the Second Vatican Council where the progressive party—to use the simplifying but convenient label—early set to work to derail the schema of a draft document entitled "On the Blessed Virgin Mary, Mother of God and Mother of Men," approved by John XXIII before the council opened in the autumn of 1962.[24] A new working title was adopted a few months later: "On the Blessed Virgin Mary, Mother of the Church": a move reflecting, evidently, acceptance of ecclesio-typicality in Mariology on the part of the Roman curia and its consultors at this date. However, the German and Austrian bishops, fearing that even under the revised title such a document would be ecumenically disadvantageous, managed to put their most able *peritus*, Karl Rahner, in charge of reworking the schema as a whole. It was Rahner's idea that the text should be reduced to the status of a chapter within *Lumen gentium,* the Dogmatic Constitution of the Council on the Church. A signal was needed by Protestant ecclesial communities that Catholics were serious about what was termed "Marian reform."

The phrase "Marian reform" covered a multitude of sins. It included at least three elements: the suppression of what were deemed

---

24. I use in this section the anonymous article entitled "'Behold your Mother': A reconsideration of Mary's relationship to the Church in the light of the Vatican II debate over *Lumen gentium* and Paul VI's decision to intervene," published in *Inside the Vatican* (April 1996): 249–53.

superstitious aspects of popular piety; the alleged incompatibility of Marian devotional exercises, notably the Rosary, with a reassertion of the priority of liturgical prayer; and the objections of representatives of the *ressourcement* movements in biblical and patristic studies to the form taken by much of the later Marian theology in the church.

Above all, supporters of Marian reform were adamant that, in Rahner's words, the council should avoid stirring up "new difficulties and dangers" by proceeding to doctrinal definitions of, or even the making of large statements about, Marian mediation—Mary's role in the objective and subjective redemption. Conservative bishops, notably from Italy, started to complain that the ecumenical obsessions of some of their colleagues were making it impossible to speak of traditional Catholic doctrines concerning our Lady. The final version of the Marian schema, the eighth chapter of *Lumen gentium* was eventually passed by a margin of only seventeen votes in a gathering where over two thousand bishops were present: by far the closest call of any decision made at Vatican II.

What, however, surprised or even dismayed many moderates in the conciliar assembly was the rejection of the revised title "Mother of the Church" by a now revamped theological commission on which curialists were obliged to take a back seat. In the late autumn of 1964 Paul VI decided to intervene. On the feast of Mary's Presentation in the Temple, appealing to his personal authority as successor to Peter, he bestowed on her the title *mater ecclesiae* by his own hand. Making his announcement to the assembly, Paul VI declared:

> For the glory of the Virgin Mary and for our own consolation, we proclaim the most holy Mary as Mother of the Church, that is to say, of all the People of God. . . . And we wish from now on that the Virgin should be still more honored and invoked by the entire people under this most dear title.

But the title was not "most dear" to absolutely everyone. The Protestant observers, wrote the Vaticanologist Peter Hebblethwaite, were not amused, and he reported that applause in the aula was limited to the conciliar minority. Another priest journalist, Francis Xavier Murphy, writing from a position of sympathy with the progressive party, went further. "[T]he grim-faced pope was carried out of the basilica through . . . tiers of stony-faced, unresponsive bishops, whose lack of enthusiasm was the dominant note of the proceedings." The Verbist Ralph Wiltgren, coming at events from another theological standpoint, seems to be describing a different scene. "The standing ovation which greeted this announcement signified the warm assent of the Council Fathers."[25]

Ironically, the most distinguished of the Protestant observers whom the announcement discomfited, the Swiss Reformed exegete-theologian Oscar Cullmann, had also felt negative about Rahner's darling, *Lumen gentium* 8. It was, he considered, a gun that had backfired. As he put it: "A decision which was in fact intended to weaken Mariology has in reality made it stronger, because everything about the church culminates, so to speak, in this chapter."[26]

But here we must leave the voices at the conciliar event, and instead note how Scheffczyk—thirty years later, and acting as coeditor of a six-volume German-language Marian encyclopedia—gave himself the task of writing the article on Mary at the Second Vatican Council. He took the opportunity to speak of what he considered the "stinginess and reticence" of the Constitution's eighth chapter. That was to be explained, Scheffczyk went on, "as is openly admitted, by showing consideration for ecumenical dialogue, especially with Protestants." But this, he concluded tersely, "does not stop theology from saying more."[27]

25. See note 24 above.
26. See note 24 above, p. 249.

To put it in terms that have since become familiar: here, as with everything concerning the council, we must read texts according to a hermeneutic of continuity, not a hermeneutic of discontinuity and rupture.

27. In *Marienlexikon*, ed. Remigius Baümer and Leo Scheffczyk, 6 vols. (Sankt Ottilien, Germany: EOS Verlag, 1988–1994), II, 571.

8

An Excursus on Eastern Orthodox Theology and Marian Art

With the very minor exceptions of some Western rite Orthodox communities in France and the United States of America, Orthodoxy uses the Byzantine liturgy for its worship, and that liturgy, and its accompanying iconography, plays a relatively much larger role in Orthodox Mariology than does the equivalent in Catholic Marian thought.[1] Moreover, Orthodox Mariology is much less likely than Catholic to take the form of systematically focused treatises on the Mother of the Lord, a reflection of the weaker influence of Scholasticism in late medieval Byzantium and early modern and modern (prerevolutionary) Russia. The influence of that highly organized approach to Christian thinking was feebler in the East, though certainly not nonexistent. In our contemporary period, the tone of Orthodox theological writing is generally more spiritual, and

---

1. Louis Bouyer, "Le culte de Marie dans la liturgie byzantine," *Maison-Dieu* 38 (1954): 122–135.

less academic, when compared with what is customary in the Latin Church, despite the mixed fortunes of Scholasticism since the Second Vatican Council.

The Divine Motherhood

Given this background, it seems appropriate enough to start out from the hymn to the Mother of God in the Liturgy of St. John Chrysostom. It is a hymn which follows immediately upon the eucharistic consecration, and precedes the reading of the diptychs when the names of the saints of the day are read out, and the departed prayed for, along with various categories of the living. The rationale for this arrangement is that the Lord's presence on the altar, newly achieved in the transformation worked at the consecration, compels, as it were, the worshipping church to remember the entire ecclesial body of Christ.

> It is truly right to bless you, O God-bearing one, as the ever-blessed and immaculate Mother of our God. More honourable than the cherubim and by far more glorious than the seraphim. Ever a virgin you gave birth to God the Word; O true Mother of God, we magnify you.

This short text finds illustration in the sixteenth-century icon *It Is Truly Right to Glorify You* in the Dormition Cathedral of the Moscow Kremlin where, in the top two and the bottom right segments, citations from this hymn are held out—by angels in the first two cases, by the church doctors Cyril of Alexandria and Basil the Great in the third. Meanwhile, the top left segment shows angels surrounding the *Theotokos* who is enthroned with her Child: they are worshipping together with the representatives of humankind depicted below. The bottom left segment which portrays the Mother and Child in a triple geometrical figure—two stars and a circle, indicating the Holy Spirit, the Son, and the Father—is itself divided into nine squares filled with angelic forms. These correspond to the nine levels of angelic dignity identified in the little treatise *On the Celestial Hierarchy* by the sixth-century Syrian monk who took the nom-de-plume Denys the Areopagite. What we are being told is that, thanks to Mary's relation with her Child, the Mother of the Lord is exalted above the entire intellectual creation—including over all those human beings who have been deified—fully sanctified—through receiving God's grace.

The claim thus made in visual images is the equivalent to the claim of Thomistic Mariology, which we visited in chapter two, to the effect that Mary alone of creatures has entered the hypostatic order—the order of the Trinitarian hypostases. In this sense, she is raised above not only the highest kinds of natural reality but above even the order of grace itself. She is indeed, therefore, "by far more glorious than the seraphim."

The threefold reference in this short hymn to Mary's bearing the Word, along with the prominent role given in this icon to St. Cyril, suggests how Orthodoxy is, so to speak, continuously at war with Nestorianism—which is also why the advent of a low Christology in some Catholic circles in the post-conciliar West can be said to pose a fresh ecumenical obstacle in Catholic-Orthodox relations. (Not that a high Christology—such as, for example, Barthians, maintain—leads necessarily to a strongly developed Mariological doctrine and devotion.)

The Russian émigré theologian Vladimir Lossky wrote in 1949 that were the Orthodox to limit themselves to the dogmatic data defined by the councils, the only thing they would be able to say about Mary is that she is the Mother of God. However, he goes on:

> We know instances of Christians who, while recognizing for purely Christological reasons the divine maternity of the Holy Virgin abstain from all special devotion to the Mother of God for the same

[Christological] reasons, desiring to know no other Mediator between God and man save the God-man Jesus Christ.[2]

This suffices to prove, Lossky concludes, that the Ephesian dogma by itself would not be enough to justify the unique position the Orthodox Church accords to Mary. Here the "data of dogma," as he puts it, must not be separated from the "data" of the church's cultus, i.e., the church's devotion as found in tradition.

Mary's Perpetual Virginity

No better example of that devotion can be found than the so-called Akathist Hymn, recited standing—hence its name, "a-kathistos," that is, not while sitting down, a recollection of the all-night vigil during which it was first, reputedly, sung in thanksgiving for the lifting of a siege of Constantinople by a potentially lethal combination of pagan forces, Avar, Slav, and Persian, in 626. Nowadays, the Akathist Hymn is sung in the Byzantine liturgy on the fourth Saturday of Lent, the "Saturday of the Akathist."

Described by the *Oxford Dictionary of Byzantium* as a "subtly interwoven net of images that is one of the high points of Byzantine poetry,"[3] it was a favored subject for both illuminated manuscripts and monumental wall-painting in the Middle Ages. The sixteenth-century icon *Praises of the Mother of God with Akathist* preserved in the Russian Museum in St. Petersburg shows the kind of thing: in two central ovals, one placed above the other, Jesus is portrayed linked to his mother by garlands of blue flower which represent the theme of the marriage of humanity in Mary with Mary's Son and Lord. Around them, the patriarchs and prophets along with kings

---

2. Vladimir Lossky, "Panagia," in *The Mother of God: An Anglo-Russian Symposium,* ed. E. L. Mascall (Westminster, UK: Dacre Press, 1949), 24.
3. Alexander P. Kazhdan, *The Oxford Dictionary of Byzantium* I. (New York: Oxford, 1991, 44.)

David and Solomon hold out texts and objects which anticipate the good news brought to the Virgin at the Annunciation—thus, for example, the prophet Jeremiah, shown second from the top on the left, is holding out a stone tablet, a symbol of the covenant to be made anew in Mary's Child, while his text, taken from chapter thirty-one of the Book of Jeremiah, reads, "Behold the days will come—says the Lord—when I will make a new covenant with the house of Israel and the house of Judah" (Jer. 31:31). Opposite Jeremiah is the patriarch Jacob with the ladder on which, in a dream, he saw God joined to earth. The Genesis text he is showing to the viewer explains the object in question: "I dreamt, and I saw a ladder resting on the earth, while the top reached heaven" (cf. Gen. 28:12). The covenant in question (compare Jeremiah) depends in fact on the incarnation.

The twenty-four rectangular scenes arranged around the borders of the icon named correspond to the twenty-four stanzas of the Akathist. Twelve of these rehearse the biblical narrative, up as far as the presentation of the child Jesus in the temple. The remaining twelve are theological reflections on the incarnation, represented in this Russian icon by various scenes depicting the interrelations of Mary, Christ, and the members of the church.

One thing the Akathist very clearly adds to the Ephesus dogma—*pace* Lossky's claim that the data of dogma in Orthodoxy would be poor without the data of the cultus—is emphasis on Mary's perpetual virginity. Each stanza of the hymn is followed by richly orchestrated greetings to Mary, all preceded by Gabriel's opening word at the Annunciation, *Chairé*, "Rejoice," and each set of such greetings is terminated by the acclamation, "Rejoice, Bride unwedded," for as stanza seventeen confesses:

O Mother of
God, we see
the best of speakers

become as mute
as fish in your
regard
for they could not explain how You
Could give birth
while remaining a virgin.

The Akathist text contains many allusions to other aspects of the mystery of Mary, and notably her mediation of grace. The claim summed up in the word *Theotokos* is, however, the controlling assertion of this liturgical form.

The Divine Motherhood and the Primary Fundamental Principle of Mariology

Mary's status as the God-bearer continued as it began: it remained the principal theme in Orthodox iconography where she is concerned. This corresponds in the East to the claim of writers like Suárez and Feckes in the West that the divine motherhood is the fundamental theological principle of all Mariology, a claim discussed in chapter seven above. Images of the Mother without the Child are, in Byzantine art, comparatively rare—though of course in iconic representations of events like the Annunciation and the dormition the Child is inevitably absent—at any rate, so far as the dormition is concerned, qua child.

The sixth-century Egyptian icon of the Virgin among the holdings of the Cleveland Museum of Art and the mural, also sixth century, of the Mother of God with saints in the church of Panagia Angeloktistos at Kiti in Cyprus show in two different media—tapestry and mosaic, respectively—the theological meaning of Mary's motherhood. That this is specifically a *divine* motherhood is conveyed visually by the solemnity of the figures, their monumental frontality, as well as by the presence of the angelic powers either as guarding (the Egyptian image) or as inclining in worship (the Cypriot image). The truly sovereign dignity of Mary, as shown here, has given images of this kind the name of *Kyriotissa* images, though they can also be described as direct representations of the dogma of the Council of Ephesus.

The single most common variant on the divine Motherhood theme in the art of the Byzantine/Slav icon is the Mother of God "pointing the way," as in the sixteenth-century *Mother of God of Smolensk*: an example of the image-type known as *Hodegetria*, "She who points the Way"—points the way precisely by indicating her Child. So far as art historians are concerned, the source of this Marian icon-type where the mother indicates the child with her hand is a now lost original from Constantinople where the name "She who points the Way" appears to have been something of a *double entendre.* The original icon, kept at a monastic church southeast of Hagia Sophia, close to the Great Palace, was painted in commemoration of a miracle when the Virgin appeared to two blind people and led them by the hand to this church where she gave them their sight. Praised by St. John Damascene, it was probably the image described as "painted by St. Luke" which chroniclers reported was stripped of gold and pearls by the Turks in 1453 and then destroyed.

If the name "Hodegetria" is deliberately ambiguous—Mary pointing to Christ who called himself "the Way" and herself the merciful mother of her clients pointing those who are blind (literally or metaphorically) to their road in life, then this icon expresses what twentieth-century Catholic theology would call both a christo-typical and an ecclesio-typical Mariology. It shows Mary as Mother of her Son and Mary as Mother of the Church.

Evidently, Mary's hand pointing is the focus of this ambiguity that is absent in a work which in other respects resembles it, the celebrated Roman icon called "Salvation of the Roman People," *salus populi romani*, in whose presence Pius XII defined the assumption dogma in 1950.

The Mother of God *Hodegetria* and indeed the *Salus populi romani* image are already a step away from what we might call the "Ephesian" Mother of God in Majesty, as found in the Egyptian tapestery and the Cypriot mosaic. Another sixteenth-century Russian icon, the Korsun Mother of God, by bringing the face of the Son to touch the face of the Mother while, at the same time, not abandoning the pointing gesture of the *Hodegetria*, takes us further towards an iconography of the God-bearer as an imagery of love. Hence the Russian name for this kind of icon, The Mother of God *Umilenye*, usually translated "tenderness." The word may perhaps better be rendered by the more biblical term "loving kindness," suggesting as this does participation in a divine attribute, the equivalent of the Hebrew *chesed*, and not simply the exaltation of a human sentiment. The more celebrated icon of the Vladimir Mother of God, thought to have been brought from Constantinople to Kiev around 1130, can be regarded as another example of this type.

I mentioned that the original Constantinopolitan *Hodegetria* was believed to have been painted by the evangelist Luke. The first appearance of the claim that St. Luke painted an image of Mary is in an early Byzantine chronicle of around 550. In what some scholars take to be an interpolated passage, the co-empress Pulcheria sends the icon from Jerusalem to the east Roman capital via her sister-in-law Eudoxia, the wife of the emperor Theodosius II. There are three things of interest connected with the somewhat implausible claim to Lukan provenance of this icon. First, for the Byzantines (including the Romans of the patristic period) as for the Orthodox Slavs later, a copy of a copy was regarded as equally Lukan with the original: this is sometimes referred to as the "principle of transferred apostolicity." In other words, that there are many icons claiming

Luke as artist is a way of saying that a Luke-painted image was itself copied and multiply recopied. Secondly, though the New Testament associates Luke only with the medical profession, twentieth-century exegetes have sometimes commented on the pictorial character of his imagination. His gospel proceeds for the most part by vignettes. The Lucan infancy gospel where most of his Marian material appears is perhaps the most obvious example: here was a painterly imagination in literary act. Thirdly, only *Hodegetria*-type images, defined broadly enough to include, the Roman *Salus populi romani*, are ever ascribed to St. Luke. The belief that a number of Marian images had a Lukan prototype is, consequently, intelligible—and long lasting. The late seventeenth-century Serbian painting by Master Apsalon, at Morača, in Montenegro, shows a *Hodegetria*-icon taking shape on Luke's easel.[4]

I said that the Akathist Hymn clearly adds to Lossky's minimal dogmatic datum of Mary's divine motherhood acceptance of her perpetual virginity. She is the bride unwedded. As in the Latin West, the Isaiah text (7:14) prophesying that a virgin—thus the Septuagint—will conceive played a central role here, but in the East this was in close association with the icon-type called "The Mother of God of the Sign." The young woman of the scroll of Isaiah who conceives and bears a son and calls his name "Immanuel" is the *sign* the Lord will give. The icon of our Lady of the Sign shows the Mother of God as an "orant," someone praying, with on her breast, or perhaps in her womb, the Son, the second divine person, in a circle of glory that symbolizes his divine hypostasis which is now humanized in her. In his closing speech at Ephesus, Cyril had celebrated the *Theotokos* whose immaculate womb had carried the Immense and Incomprehensible One, and this—the Virgin Mother carrying within

---

4. Gisela Kraut, *Lukas malt die Madonna: Zeugnisse zum künstlerischen Selbstverständnis in der Malerei* (Worms: Werner, 1986).

her the Logos made man—was the image decided on for the imperial chapel built at Constantinople to house the *maphorion*—the robe or veil of Mary brought from Jerusalem under the fifth-century emperor Leo I (something I had occasion to refer to in the chapter on the assumption).

The icon was copied throughout the empire and beyond. By the eleventh century it is found as far west as Torcello in the lagoon of Venice, and as far north as Kiev. In Russia, this image, as a sign of the specifically *virginal* motherhood of Mary was given particular prominence in the developed icon screen, the iconostasis, which by the sixteenth century reached from ceiling to floor in many Orthodox churches.[5] The top level of the full iconostasis is given over to the prophets (including the prophet-kings David and Solomon) but, customarily, Isaiah is omitted and in his place is depicted the realization of this particular prophecy, the "Mother of God of the Sign."

The Immaculate Conception

The Akathist is filled with references not only to the perpetual virginity of Mary, which in later Byzantine iconography is expressed in three stars on Mary's robe and veil, but also to her immaculate state before God. Stanza nineteen, for example, addresses her as *Achrante*, "O Immaculate One." In the third chapter we saw how the conviction of the *Philotheotokoi* that Mary is all-immaculate was transmitted liturgically to the West. There it passed through the crucible of theological controversy based on Paul's teaching about the universality of the need for redemption before it triumphed in the doctrine of Mary's unique mode of redemption, as expressed in

---

5. Christopher Walter, "The Origins of the Iconostasis," in idem., *Studies in Byzantine Iconography* (London: [Variorum Reprints], 1977), III.

her conception. Catholic historians who, so far as I can see, are not obviously wrong, claim that the early fourteenth-century Byzantine historian Nicephorus Kallistos Xanthopoulos was the first figure in the Greek East to set a question mark against Mary's immaculacy. Xanthopoulos, who wrote a commentary on the *Orations* of Gregory Nazianzen ("Gregory the Theologian"), had noted that for Gregory the Holy Spirit "pre-purified" the Virgin, body and soul, at the Annunciation. But whereas for Gregory to "pre-purify" implies the removal of some obstacle, his text does not actually state that this was moral stain. The *Philotheotokoi* had understood Mary's pre-purification to be either her further sanctification (as with Sophronius of Jerusalem) or the action by which in virginally conceiving the Logos she was introduced to the realm of the divine persons (as with John of Damascus).

At first, Xanthopoulos's opinion remained isolated, his better known contemporary Nicholas Cabasilas writing, for example:

> If some holy doctors said that the Virgin had been previously purified by the Spirit, we must believe they understood this purification in the sense of an augmentation of graces. Nothing in her demanded purification.[6]

In the sixteenth century, however, a conscious movement of Byzantine Maculism arose, fuelled by tension with the Latin West. For John Nathanael, for example, rector of San Giorgio dei greci at Venice, and writing in 1574, Mary became immaculate at the Annunciation. The Annunciation icon then becomes, on this view, the true icon of her all-purity.[7] Though, under Greek influence, the Russian Church adopted a similarly anti-Immaculist tone (in 1884, the Holy Synod would officially include the immaculate conception

---

6. Nicholas Cabasilas, *Homily on the Nativity of Mary*, 11.
7. See for a Catholic reading of this motif: Manuel Candal, "La Virgen santisima 'prepurificada' in su Annunciación," *Orientalia Christiana Periodica* 31 (1975): 241–276.

among the dogmatic divergences between Rome and Orthodoxy), major figures in the Russian lands dissented from the opinion expressed in this judgment. They included the influential *starets* (spiritual father) and hermit Seraphim of Sarov, whose canonization, attended by Nicholas II, was one of the last great spectacles of Russian Orthodoxy under the Tsardom.

For a modern Russian dogmatician like Lossky, where Immaculist opinion goes wrong is in ascribing to Mary a condition analogous to that of Eve before the fall. She was not, explains Lossky, a child of paradise. Rather, she was the highest peak of Old Testament holiness, which is a holiness pertaining precisely to a fallen humanity, though he hastens to add she "was to realize in her person all the holiness of which the Church is capable."[8] But, as we saw in chapter three, Mary's immaculate conception should be understood, even (or especially) by Catholics, not as return to Eden but as qualifying her for entering more deeply into the redemptive mission of her Son.

Modern Orthodox Maculism, though otherwise regrettable, has had the positive side-effect of encouraging a profound Marian theology of the Annunciation when, as for Lossky's fellow-exile Georges Florovsky, Mary is said to enjoy an "anticipated Pentecost." As the "Mother of the New Man," she has, Florovsky wrote, her "anticipated share in this very newness": Jesus rendered Son of God "in power" by the Holy Spirit and "pneumatising" the humanity of the redeemed.[9] So what happened to the apostles at Pentecost happened at the Annunciation to her.

---

8. Lossky, "Panagia," 34.
9. George Florovsky, "The Ever-Virgin Mother of God," in *The Mother of God,* ed. Mascall, 51–63, and here at 56.

Mary at the Cross: Eastern Witnesses to Co-redemption

When describing the *Hodegetria* icon I touched on the much loved and frequently reproduced image of our Lady of Vladimir. In that image, the eye of the Virgin seems to pierce the future with anguish. This brings me to the Marian icons of the passion, the "Mother of God *Strastnaia*" (the Russian word for the passion of Christ). Here the Mother and Child are flanked by angels carrying instruments of the passion to which the Child looks with a sort of fascinated foreboding while his mother engages the spectator in a steady gaze that is filled with sadness. Could this be called an icon of Marian co-redemption? Possibly it could, especially if we feel able to say that the content of the look of the Son and the Mother, once theologically interpreted, is the same. Certainly, the classical Byzantine and Russian images of the Crucified Christ with Mary and John include Mary's replicating the hand movement which is typical of the divine motherhood image of the *Hodegetria*. And this suggests that her role in bearing the Christ child and showing him to the witnesses of the infancy gospels, is resumed in climactic form at the cross.

Whether there *is* a tacit co-redemption doctrine in the Orthodox liturgy turns on how one interprets a host of texts dealing with Mary's mediation—which, as we saw in chapter six, can either be a matter of Mary's share in objective redemption (the constituting of the reality of the redemption, at incarnation and atonement), or of her share in subjective redemption (the subsequent distribution of the fruits of salvation won on the victorious cross).

The Assumption as Dormition
and Share in the Resurrection Triumph

Following the order of this book which is, broadly speaking, the order of the storyline of Mary's life, I pass now to images of the assumption in the Orthodox world. The Byzantine liturgical tradition is unanimous that after her death the Mother of God was given the grace of sharing to the full in the resurrection and ascension of her Son. Not for nothing does the Greek Church call the assumption festival the "Easter of summertime." A *kontakion* for August 15 runs: "The tomb and death could not hold the Mother of God, unceasing in her intercession and unfailing hope of patronage, for, as the Mother of life, she was transferred to life by him who had dwelt in her ever-virgin womb."

Two points are, however, worth making. First, while the Orthodox objection to Pius XII's dogmatization of the assumption chiefly concerned the manner of the definition—both its papal, rather than conciliar, form and in the way the bull *Munificentissimus Deus* linked the assumption to the immaculate conception, there was also some anxiety about the content of the definition inasmuch as the pope left open the question, "Did Mary actually die?." That is a question the Byzantine liturgy answers with a resounding "Yes!." I said in the fourth chapter that in modern Western Mariology there is a thesis (possessed of some—but, it has to be said, very modest—patristic anticipation), according to which Mary did not in fact die. Pius XII, following in this the Western practice in doctrinal definition, was reluctant to exclude a position hitherto regarded as fully legitimate, though in no way commanding a consensus in the theological schools.

My second point about the Orthodox attitude to the assumption dogma concerns the role of the *Transitus* accounts. In chapter four,

I reported that in the build-up to the definition, Immortalists (those who said Mary did not die but went immediately from life with a lower case "l" to life with an upper case "L," the Life everlasting), tended to be skeptical of the strictly historical evidence for Mary's assumption. They didn't favor giving any historical weight to the late patristic accounts of Mary's falling asleep. The *Transitus Mariae* were, after all, thoroughly Mortalist in character. Owing, however, to the place of those accounts in the Byzantine liturgy, and their citation by such Fathers as St. John of Damascus, the Orthodox traditionally pay the *Transitus* legends more respect. A prayer on the Dormition feast runs for example: "Although she was buried in a grave of corruption, you lifted her on high in a manner beyond our understanding and gathered your apostles from everywhere to be at her tomb." That refers to a motif—the assembly of the apostles at Mary's deathbed—often found in the *Transitus* narratives. In the classic Byzantine-Slav icon of the dormition the apostles are grouped, accordingly, on either side of Mary's bed.

It is pertinent to Orthodox iconography to observe that one of the main questions differentiating the various *Transitus* accounts is whether, at the dormition, the Lord brought Mary's body to the same state as her soul, or whether, as in some versions, a certain disjunction remained—her body transferred to beneath the Tree of Life in paradise, understood as a place of waiting for the resurrection of the just, but her soul taken directly to glory. This hesitation is reflected in the classic Byzantine icon of the falling asleep, where it is the soul of Mary Christ carries in his arms, as both he and Mary's soul contemplate the body that soul has left behind.

Perhaps it could be argued that, theologically, the real Byzantine icons of the bodily assumption of Mary into glory are not the dormition icon at all but, as in the eleventh-century Byzantine image now at St. Mark's Basilica in Venice, the "Nicopeia" or Mother of

God "Bringer of Victory." Though to art historians, this is a form of the majestic Mother of God from which we started out, nevertheless, Mary's assumption is precisely about "victory." Indeed, thanks to the work of her Son, it can even be called the supreme victory over death since, as Vladimir Lossky wrote, Mary assumed into heaven embodies the passage from the church to the kingdom of God, placing her as he put it "now in this time, beyond death, beyond the resurrection, and beyond the Last Judgment."[10] She also holds out the prospect of sharing this victory with the church's other members, which brings me to the two final themes of Mary as mediatrix of graces and Mary and the church.

Mary as Mediatrix of Graces

Numerous images concern the Orthodox devotion to Mary as mediatrix of graces. In an early seventeenth-century polyptych of Christ, the Mother of God and saints in Moscow's Tretyakov Gallery, the left-hand panel contains the most obvious kind of representation of the intercession of our Lady: she holds out on an unrolled scroll the petition she is making to her Son. Note that the petition is prolonging, or confirming, the prayers of the saints who are depicted in the rest of the painting. That is a testimony to the distinction between the Mother of God and all other saints, as reflected in the qualitatively different worship given her: *hyperdulia*, not *dulia*. A joint letter of the Orthodox patriarchs of Constantinople, Alexandria and Jerusalem sought in 1718 to explain this distinction to the Anglican Non-Jurors who were putting out feelers towards Orthodoxy.

The much loved images of the Mother of God of the *Pokrov* or "Protecting Veil" reflect the distinctively Orthodox version of the

10. Lossky, "Panagia," 35.

notion of the cloak of the Mother of God, discussed in the sixth chapter of this book. That version originates with the *Vita* of the tenth-century Byzantine saint Andrew the Fool, who, according to the *Life*, with one of his disciples saw the Mother of Jesus, supported by John the Baptist and John the Evangelist, and accompanied by other saints, coming through the royal doors separating the sanctuary from the nave in the imperial church at Constantinople and covering the people with her veil or mantle. Incidentally, it is striking how many iconographic themes in Marian devotion have some link to the Byzantine capital, the Queen of Cities, which became known to Byzantines as *Theotokoupolis*, "the City of the Mother of God," not only on account of the number of its Marian sanctuaries and the preeminence of their relics and images, but also owing to a continuing memory of the origins of the Akathist in the lifting of the 626 siege when, it was believed, the Virgin had taken Constantinople under her special protection.[11]

The oldest version of the iconography of Mary as mediatrix of graces is probably, however, Mary shown as holding out her hands towards her Son in a posture of supplication. This is the *Deêsis,* "the Beseeching" or, more coolly, "the Appeal,"[12] a term transferred in late nineteenth-century Russian art history to one specific embodiment of this gesture in which Christ, as judge of mankind, is flanked by the Baptist and the Mother of God interceding with him for sinners. An appeal is being brought by the greatest born of men and women outside the kingdom (namely: John, according to a saying of Jesus)

11. Cyril Mango, "Constantinople as Theotokoupolis," in *Mother of God: Representations of the Virgin in Byzantine Art,* ed. Maria Vassilaki (Milan: Skira, 2000), 209–218; Vasiliki Limberis, *Divine Heiress: The Virgin Mary and the Creation of Christian Constantinople* (London: Taylor & Francis, 1994).
12. In Byzantine law, a chief judge of appeals, *krités epi tón deéseôn,* was established in the seventh century: see Judith Herrin, *Byzantium: The Surprising Life of a Medieval Empire* (London: Allen Lane/Penguin, 2008 [2007]), 74. Evidently, the same word is in question.

and the greatest born of men and women inside it (namely: Mary, in the judgment of tradition). The Mother with her hands held out to one side in supplication is thought to have been the principal icon of the Constantinopolitan church called the *Hagiosontissa* some hundred meters from Hagia Sophia: this is the building where there was kept the girdle of Mary, a companion relic to her robe or veil. By the sixteenth century, the *Deêsis* in the modern art-historical definition—Christ the Judge with Mary and the Baptist—had been given the place of honor in the developed Russian icon screen, just over the royal doors, the central portal to the sanctuary.

The later Byzantine image-type which hails the Mother of God under the title "Source of Life" is yet another expression of Mary as mediatrix of grace. The icon shows Mary as with her Son the source of the water of grace. Like the *Pokrov*, the Mother of God of the Protecting Veil, it commemorates a very particular expression of this universal truth—specifically, certain miracles worked at Mary's intercession at a spring by the Western gate of Constantinople. The icon portrays Mary, the infant Christ on her breast, half-immersed in a large basin from out of which jets allow liquid to run forth. Though the feast of the Mother of God Source of Life was not formally introduced into the Byzantine liturgy till the fourteenth century, its imagery is thought to have influenced the medieval Latin expressions of Mary's mediatorial role as canal, aqueduct, well, and fountain—all of which metaphors, of course, exploit the same aquatic imagery.

The icon of the Mother of God Life-giving Source seems to correspond to the high doctrine of Marian mediation we examined in the sixth chapter. In the words of Joseph Lebon, the Belgian theologian who, so we saw, composed the Roman Office of Mary Mediatrix of all Graces under Pius XI, Christ and Mary form, for this icon, "one single total principle of grace," the New Adam with the New Eve.

Mary and the Church

I said that the overwhelming predominance of Mother and Child images in the Orthodox world could count as the Byzantine equivalent of the Western *theologoumenon* that the divine motherhood is the primary fundamental principle of Mariology. But ecclesiotypical images can also be found. The twelfth-century *Maria orans* mosaic in the Basilica Ursiana at Ravenna, in northeast Italy, may seem to come from the West, but in that century Ravenna still lay within the Byzantine sphere of cultural influence, if only just. The twentieth-century Russian speculative dogmatician Sergei Bulgakov found the image of Mary alone to be an image of Mary as the personal embodiment of the church. As he wrote in his Mariological study, *The Burning Bush*:

> It would be impossible to say in so many words that Mary is the Church, and yet it may be said that the Church is represented by Mary insofar as in her person all the attributes of the Church find their personal, final, and most perfect embodiment. . . . The Mother of God is the praying Church itself in its personal embodiment.[13]

That is also expressed in a corporate manner in the Russian image called "The Synaxis of the Mother of God." This icon corresponds to the Marian feast kept on December 26 in the Byzantine rite, a feast which celebrates Mary's motherhood but in a way that affirms how all humanity is to be drawn to the Mother of the Word incarnate. The figures in conical hats at the bottom of the icon represent the wider humanity which is summoned to assembly—synaxis—along with the shepherds, higher up on the right, and the magi, facing on the left,

13. James Pain and Nicolas Zernov, eds., *A Bulgakov Anthology* (London: SPCK, 1976), 95. For an overview of Bulgakov's Mariology, see Aidan Nichols, *Wisdom from Above: A Primer in the Theology of Father Sergei Bulgakov* (Leominster: Gracewing Publishing, 2005), 240–253.

who actually came to Bethlehem, prefiguring as they did so the various conditions of human being called to enter the church. In an unexpected touch, the be-hatted figures denote humanity *in the form of a choir*, for the headgear marks them out as singers at the imperial court. The layout of the scene, with its symmetrical distribution of characters, is suggestive in fact of antiphonal singing. All ends in praise.

This image also hints at the *cosmic* character of Mary's role which is better brought out, though, as we shall shortly see, in the icon-type called "In You all Creation Rejoices." In the "Synaxis of the Mother of God," a personification of the earth, on the far left, placed behind a monk whose turban identifies him as St. John of Damascus, offers Mary a cave, while on the right a similar personification of the desert, positioned behind a contemporary of Damascene's, Cosmas of Maiuma—like him celebrated for hymns in praise of Mary—offers her a manger made of stone. Both of the objects offered—cave and stone manger—have a paschal connotation. The stone of the manger evokes the tomb hewn from rock where Christ's dead body was placed. The black, jagged outline of the cave is meant to suggest the entrance to the underworld to which on Holy Saturday he descended so as to bind the evil angels. But through the figures of earth and desert, manger and cave also represent the cosmic context of the incarnation as a whole.

The Cosmic Significance of the Mother of God

In the icon "In You All Creation Rejoices" this cosmic dimension is hugely extended. Here heaven and earth, trees and birds "rejoice" together for the Mother of God. Mary and her Son sit in a paradisal temple. She is surrounded by angelic figures representing heaven as it greets the true temple who received in her womb the Creator of the world. At the foot stands a throng of saints, prophets and apostles, bishops and martyrs, monks and hermits. The iconographer has given particular prominence to the two groups of women martyrs positioned closer to the throne of the *Theotokos* than are the others.

Georges Florovsky could be describing this wonderful icon when he closes his essay "The Ever-Virgin Mother" by situating Mary in the company of all redeemed creatures:

> And this glorious assembly, they discern the eminent person of the Virgin Mother of the Lord and Redeemer, full of grace and love, of charity and compassion—[and now quoting from the liturgical hymn with which this chapter opened] "more honourable than the cherubim, more glorious than the seraphim, who without spot didst bear the Eternal Word."[14]

14. Florovsky, "The Ever-Virgin Mother," 63.

Select Bibliography

General

Baümer, Remigius and Leo Scheffczyk, eds. *Marienlexikon.* 6 vols. Sankt Ottilien, Germany: EOS Verlag, 1988–1994.

Bouyer, Louis. *The Seat of Wisdom: An Essay on the Place of the Virgin Mary in Christian Theology.* Chicago: Pantheon Books, 1965.

Gambero, Luigi. *Mary and the Fathers of the Church: The Blessed Virgin Mary in Patristic Thought.* San Francisco: Ignatius Press, 1991.

_____. *Mary in the Middle Ages: The Blessed Virgin Mary in the Thought of Mediaeval Latin Theologians.* San Francisco: Ignatius Press, 1995.

Graef, Hilda Charlotte. *A History of Doctrine and Devotion.* 2 vols. London: Sheed and Ward, 1963 (vol. 1), 1965 (vol. 2), and 1985 (combined edition).

Laurentin, René. *Court Traité sur la théologie mariale.* 5th ed. Paris: Lethielleux, 1968.

Manoir, Hubert du, ed. *Maria: Études sur la sainte Vierge.* 8 vols. Paris: Editions Beauchesne, 1948–1971.

O'Carroll, Michael. *Theotokos: A Theological Encyclopedia of the Blessed Virgin Mary.* Collegeville, MN: Liturgical Press, 1982.

Rahner, Karl. *Mary, Mother of the Lord: Theological Meditations.* London: Herder, 1963.

Schillebeeckx, Edward. *Mary, Mother of the Redemption: The Religious Bases of the Mystery of Mary.* London: Sheed and Ward, 1964.

Chapter 1: The Blessed Virgin Mary in the New Testament

Braun, François-Marie. *La Mère des fidèles: Essai de théologie johannique.* Paris/Tournai: Casterman, 1954.

Brown, Raymond E., et al., eds. *Mary in the New Testament: A Collaborative Assessment by Protestant and Roman Catholic Scholars.* Philadelphia and New York: Paulist Press International, 1978.

Feuillet, André. "La Vierge Marie dans le Nouveau Testament," in *Maria: Études sur la sainte Vierge,* vol. 6, edited by Hubert du Manoir, 15–69. Paris: Editions Beauchesne, 1961.

_____. "Le Messie et sa mère d'après le chapitre XII de l'Apocalypse," *Revue biblique* 66 (1959), pp. 58–86, reprinted in *Études johanniques* (Paris, 1962): 272–310.

_____. "Les adieux du Christ à sa mère (Jn 19, 25-27) et la maternité spirituelle de Marie," in *Nouvelle revue théologique* 86 (1964): 469–489.

Laurentin, René. *Structure et théologie de Luc 1–2.* Paris: Gabalda, 1957.

_____. *Jésus et le Temple: Mystère de Pâques et foi de Marie en Luc 1–2.* Paris: Gabalda, 1966.

Legrand, Lucien. *L'Annonce à Marie (Lc 1, 26–38): Une apocalypse aux origines de l'Evangile.* Paris: Cerf, 1981.

McHugh, John. *The Mother of Jesus in the New Testament.* London: Doubleday, 1975.

Mussner, Franz. *Maria, die Mutter Jesu im Neuen Testament.* Sankt Ottilien, Germany: EOS Verlag, 1993.

Pelikan, Jaroslav. "Miriam of Nazareth in the New Testament," in *Mary through the Centuries: Her Place in the History of Culture.* 7–22. New Haven, CT: Yale University Press, 1996.

de la Potterie, Ignace. *Mary in the Mystery of the Covenant.* Translated by Bertrand Buby. Staten Island, NY: Alba House, 1992.

Chapter 2: The Divine Motherhood

de Aldama, José Antonio. "La maternité virginale de Notre Dame," in *Maria: Études sur la sainte Vierge,* vol. 7, edited by Hubert du Manoir, 117–152. Paris: Editions Beauchesne, 1964.

Manteau-Bonamy, H. M. *Maternité divine et incarnation: Étude historique et doctrinale de Saint Thomas à nos jours.* Paris: J. Vrin, 1949.

McGuckin, John Anthony. *Saint Cyril of Alexandria and the Christological Controversy.* Crestwood, NY: St Vladimir's Seminary Press, 2004.

Mercenier, F. "L'antienne mariale grecque la plus ancienne," *Le Muséon* 52 (1939): 229–233.

Nicolas, Marie-Joseph. "Essai de synthèse mariale," in *Maria: Études sur la sainte Vierge,* vol. 1, edited by Hubert du Manoir, 707–741. Paris: Editions Beauchesne, 1948.

Pelikan, Jaroslav. "Theotokos," in *Mary through the Centuries: Her Place in the History of Culture.* 60–69. New Haven, CT: Yale University Press, 1996.

Chapter 3: The Immaculate Conception

Galot, Jean. "L'Immaculée Conception," in *Maria: Études sur la sainte Vierge,* vol. 7, edited by Hubert du Manoir, 9–116. Paris: Editions Beauchesne, 1964.

Guérard des Lauriers, Michel Louis. "L'Immaculée Conception, clé des privilèges de Marie," *Revue thomiste* 56 (1956): 43–87.

Horst, Ulrich. *Die Diskussion um die Immaculata Conceptio im Dominikanerorde.* Paderborn, Germany: F. Schöningh, 1987.

Jugie, Martin. *L'Immaculée Conception dans l'Écriture sainte et dans la Tradition orientale.* Rome: Franciscan Institute Publications, 1952.

Lamy, Marielle. *L'Immaculée Conception: étapes et enjeux d'une controverse au Moyen Âge [XIIe–XVe siècles].* Paris: Institut d'Études Augustiniennes, 2000.

O'Connor, Edward Dennis, ed. *The Dogma of the Immaculate Conception: History and Significance.* Notre Dame, IN: University of Notre Dame Press, 1958.

Chapter 4: The Co-redemptrix

Dissard, Jean. "La transfixion de Notre Dame." In *Études* 155 (1918): 257–286.

Dubarle, André M. "Les fondements bibliques du titre mariale de Nouvelle Eve." In *Recherches de science religieuse* 39 (1951), = *Mélanges Jules Lebreton* I: 49–64.

Druwé, E. "La médiation universelle de Marie," in *Maria: Études sur la sainte Vierge,* vol. 1, edited by Hubert du Manoir, 417–452. Paris: Editions Beauchesne, 1948.

de Koninck, Charles. "The Immaculate Conception and the Divine Motherhood, Assumption and Coredemption," in *The Dogma of the Immaculate Conception: History and Significance,* edited by E. D. O'Connor, 363–412. Notre Dame, IN: University of Notre Dame Press, 1958.

Miravalle, Mark, ed. *Mary: Coredemptrix, Mediatrix, Advocate: Theological Foundations: Towards a Papal Definition?* Santa Barbara, CA: Queenship, 1995.

Smith, George D. *Mary's Part in Our Redemption.* 2nd ed. London: Burns and Oates, 1955.

Chapter 5: The Assumption

Burghardt, Walter J. *The Testimony of the Patristic Age concerning Mary's Death.* Westminster, MD: The Newman Press, 1957.

Capelle, Bernard. "Théologie de l'Assomption d'après le Bulle *Munificentissimus Deus.*" *Nouvelle revue théologique* 72 (1950): 1009–1027

Daley, Brian E. *On the Dormition of Mary: Early Patristic Homilies.* Crestwood, NY: St. Vladimir's Seminary Press, 1998.

Friethoff, Caspar. "The Dogmatic Definition of the Assumption." *The Thomist* 14 (1951): 41–58.

Galot, Jean. "Le mystère de l'Assomption," in *Maria: Études sur la sainte Vierge,* vol. 7, edited by Hubert du Manoir, 153-237. Paris: Editions Beauchesne, 1964.

Healey, Kilian. "The Assumption among Mary's Privileges," *The Thomist* 14 (1951): 72-92.

Jugie, Martin. *La mort et l'assomption de la Sainte Vierge: Étudehistoric-doctrinale.* Rome: Biblioteca Apostolica Vaticana, 1944.

_____. "Assomption de la Sainte Vierge," in *Maria: Études sur la sainte Vierge,* vol. 1, edited by Hubert du Manoir, 619–658. Paris: Editions Beauchesne, 1948.

Shoemaker, Stephen J. *Ancient Traditions of the Virgin Mary's Dormition and Assumption.* Oxford: Oxford University Press, 2002.

Wenger, Antoine. *L'Assomption de la T. S. Vierge dans la tradition byzantine du VIe au Xe siècle.* Paris: Institut Français d'Études Byzantines, 1955.

Chapter 6: Mediatrix of Graces

Delaney, John J., ed. *A Woman Clothed with the Sun: Eight Great Apparitions of Our Lady in Modern Times.* New York: Image, 1960.

Gillet, Henry Martin. *Famous Shrines of Our Lady.* 2 vols. London: Newman Press, 1949–1953.

Holstein, Henri. "Les apparitions mariales," in *Maria: Études sur la sainte Vierge,* vol. 5, edited by Hubert du Manoir, 757–778. Paris: Editions Beauchesne, 1964.

Laurentin, René. *The Apparitions of the Blessed Virgin Mary Today.* Translated by Luke Griffin. Dublin: Veritas Publications, 1991.

Lebon, Joseph. "L'apostolicité de la doctrine de la médiation mariale," *Recherches de théologie ancienne et médiévale* 2 (1930): 129–159.

_____. "Comment je conçois, j'établis et je défends la doctrine de la médiation mariale," *Ephemerides theologicae lovanienses* 16 (1939): 655–744.

Miravalle, Mark, ed. *Mary: Coredemptrix, Mediatrix, Advocate: Theological Foundations: Towards a Papal Definition?* Santa Barbara, CA: Queenship, 1995.

Nolan, Mary Lee and Sidney Nolan. *Christian Pilgrimage in Modern Western Europe.* Chapel Hill, NC: University of North Carolina Press, 1989.

Smith, George D. *Mary's Part in our Redemption.* London: Burns and Oates, 1955.

Zimdars-Swartz, Sandra L. *Encountering Mary: From La Salette to Medjugorje.* Princeton, NJ: Princeton University Press, 1991.

Chapter 7: Our Lady and the Church

Coathalem, Hervé. *Le Parallelisme entre la sainte Vierge et l'église dans la tradition Latine jusqu'á la fin du XIIe siècle.* Rome: Analecta Gregoriana, 1954.

Deiss, Lucien. *Marie, fille de Sion.* Paris: Desclée de Brouwer, 1959.

Dillenschneider, Clément. *Le principe premier d'une théologie mariale organique: Orientations.* Paris: Editions Alsatia, 1955.

Feckes, Carl. "Das Fundamentalprinzip der Mariologie," in *Scientia Sacra: Festschrift für Kardinal Schulte*, 252–276. Cologne-Dusseldorf: J. P. Bachem, 1935.

Müller, Aloys. *Ecclesia-Maria: Die Einheit Marias und der Kirche.* Freiburg in der Schweiz: Editions Universitaires, 1951.

_____. "Um die Grundlagen der Mariologie," *Divus Thomas* (Freiburg) 29 (1951): 384–402.

Patfoort, Albert. "'Le' principe premier de la Mariologie?," *Revue des sciences philosophiques et théologiques* 41 (1957): 445–454.

Philips, Gérard. "Marie et l'Église, un thème théologique renouvelé," in *Maria: Études sur la sainte Vierge,* vol. 7, edited by Hubert du Manoir, 363–420. Paris: Editions Beauchesne, 1964.

Rahner, Hugo. *Our Lady and the Church.* 1961. Reprint, San Francisco: Zaccheus Press, 2005.

Scheffczyk, Leo. *Das Mariengeheimnis in Frömmigkeit und Lehre der Karolingerzeit.* Leipzig: Erfurter Theologische Studien, 1959.

Semmelroth, Otto. *Mary Archetype of the Church: The Organic Construction of the Mystery of Mary.* Dublin: Gill & Son, 1964.

Chapter 8: Excursus on
Eastern Orthodox Theology and Marian Art

Balić, Charles. "L'Immaculée Conception de Marie dans la théologie contemporaine serbe-orthodoxe," *Revue des études byzantines* 11 (1953, = Mélanges Martin Jugie): 34–46.

Bouyer, Louis. "Le culte de Marie dans la liturgie byzantine," *Maison-Dieu* 38 (1954): 122–135.

Florovsky, George. "The Ever-Virgin Mother of God," in *The Mother of God: An Anglo-Russian Symposium,* edited by E. L. Mascall, 51–63. Westminster, UK: Dacre Press, 1949.

Gordillo, Mauricius. *Mariologia orientalis.* Rome: Pont. Institutum Orientalium Studiorum, 1954.

Jugie, Martin. "L'Immaculée Conception dans l'Église grecque après le Concile d'Ephèse," in *Dictionnaire de théologie catholique* VII/1. Paris: Librairie Letouzey et Ané, 1927.

Limberis, Vasiliki. *Divine Heiress: The Virgin Mary and the Creation of Christian Constantinople.* London: Routledge, 1994.

Lossky, Vladimir. "Panagia," in *The Mother of God: An Anglo-Russian Symposium,* edited by E. L. Mascall, 24–36. Westminster, UK: Dacre Press, 1949.

Lossky, Vladimir and Leonid Ouspensky. *The Meaning of Icons.* Crestwood, NY: St. Vladimir's Seminary Press, 1982.

Nissiotis, Nikos. "Maria in der orthodoxen Theologie der Ostkirche," in *Was geht uns Maria an? Beiträge zur Auseinandersetzung in Theologie, Kirche, und Frömmigkeit,* edited by Moltmann-Wendel, 88–111. 2nd edition. Gütersloh: Gütersloher Verlagshaus Mohn, 1991.

Rouët de Journel, Marie Joseph. "Marie et l'iconographie russe," in *Maria: Études sur la sainte Vierge,* vol. 2, edited by Hubert du Manoir, 445–481. Paris: Editions Beauchesne, 1949.

Sirota, Ioann B. *Die Ikonographie der Gottesmutter in der Russischen Orthodoxen Kirche: Versuch einer Systematisierung.* Würzburg: Augustinus-Verlag, 1992.

Stiernon, David. "Marie dans la théologie orthodoxe gréco-russe," in *Maria: Études sur la sainte Vierge,* vol. 7, edited by Hubert du Manoir, 239–338. Paris: Editions Beauchesne, 1964.

Vassilaki, Maria, ed. *Mother of God: Representations of the Virgin in Byzantine Art.* Milan: Skira, 2000.

Vloberg, Maurice. "Les types iconographiques de la Mère de Dieu dans l'art byzantin," in *Maria: Études sur la sainte Vierge,* vol. 2, edited by Hubert du Manoir, 403–443. Paris: Editions Beauchesne, 1949.

Walter, Christopher. "Two Notes on the Deesis," in *Revue des études byzantines* 26 (1968): 326–336.

Index of Names